The Guided Reading

KIDSTATION
MODEL

Making Instruction Meaningful for the Whole Class

E. Francine Guastello & Claire R. Lenz

INTERNATIONAL
Reading Association
800 BARKSDALE ROAD, PO BOX 8139
NEWARK, DE 19714-8139, USA
www.reading.org

LAP
G934
2007

Executive Editor, Books   Corinne M. Mooney
Developmental Editor   Charlene M. Nichols
Developmental Editor   Tori Mello Bachman
Developmental Editor   Stacey Lynn Sharp
Editorial Production Manager   Shannon T. Fortner
Design and Composition Manager   Anette Schuetz

Project Editors   Charlene M. Nichols and Rebecca A. Fetterolf

Cover   Design, Paula Sloman; Photograph, © iStockphoto.com

Library of Congress Cataloging-in-Publication Data

Guastello, E. Francine, 1952-
   The guided reading kidstation model : making instruction meaningful for the whole class / E. Francine Guastello & Claire R. Lenz.
       p. cm.
   Includes bibliographical references and index.
   ISBN 978-0-87207-680-8
   1. Guided reading. 2. Group reading. I. Lenz, Claire R., 1942- II. Title.
   LB1050.377.G83 2007
   372.41'64--dc22
                                                                    2007022610

To Josephine Gemake, whose enthusiasm for teaching has been my source of inspiration both personally and professionally, and to Richard Sinatra, whose work ethic keeps me writing

—Fran

To my husband, Henry, and my children, Denise, Daniel, and Cynthia, for their love and encouragement

—Claire

CONTENTS

Francine Guastello is an associate professor of literacy and coordinator of the graduate literacy program at St. John's University, Jamaica, New York, USA. She is also the chair of the School of Education's Curriculum Committee. Fran is a two-time recipient of a federal grant under Title II-A of the No Child Left Behind Act, whereby she works by day in inner-city  elementary schools with ongoing staff development and classroom demonstrations. She is the supervisor and instructor for the Graduate Literacy Practicum Program, also servicing diverse learners in the inner-city schools.

Fran is a fellow in the Orton Gillingham Academy of Practitioners and Educators and has initiated the first Orton-Gillingham Multisensory Approach to Language Learning training in the university. Prior to becoming a university professor, Fran was an elementary school teacher for 12 years, a principal for 16 years, and an adjunct professor of literacy at Fordham and St. John's universities.

Her research interests and numerous professional publications include topics that focus on effective instructional practice for literacy development for low-achieving schools, improving the learning experiences of diverse learners, and the promotion of family literacy.

Author Information for Correspondence and Workshops

Please contact me at St. John's University, 8000 Utopia Parkway, Jamaica, NY 11439. I can also be reached by e-mail at DrFranG@aol.com or Guastelf@stjohns.edu.

Claire R. Lenz is the director of the graduate program in literacy and cognition in the Child Development Department at St. Joseph's College, Patchogue, New York, USA. Claire also served as an adjunct assistant professor of literacy at St. John's University. She is a past president of the St. John's Chapter of Phi Delta Kappa. Claire has written articles, presented at conferences, and conducted workshops on teaching literacy in the elementary school. In her 34-year career in public education, she served as a classroom teacher, reading resource teacher, teacher of the gifted, curriculum supervisor, assistant principal, and principal. Currently, she enjoys working with undergraduate and graduate students, preparing them for their roles as classroom teachers of literacy or literacy specialists.

Claire has conducted research on numerous topics related to literacy including family literacy, parents as writing partners, the effect of attitude and motivation on reading achievement, as well as how to improve reading and writing skills in low-performing schools. Presently, she is conducting research and investigating how the brain functions during reading and writing processes with the implications for effective instruction.

Author Information for Correspondence and Workshops

Please contact me at St. Joseph's College, 155 West Roe Boulevard, Patchogue, NY 11772. I can also be reached by e-mail at clenz@sjcny.edu.

PREFACE

ost elementary-grade classroom teachers work diligently to plan and implement a balanced literacy program so they can provide for the needs of each of their students. This task can be daunting in light of meeting state proficiency standards and preparing students to be successful on standardized tests in English language arts. Although modeled reading, shared reading, independent reading, and read-aloud are important components in a balanced literacy program, guided reading is its heart. Through guided reading, the teacher can determine each student's strengths and needs by delivering instruction and reinforcement for specific developmental levels. One of the most common difficulties teachers experience is how to carve out enough time during the instructional day to give quality instruction to each guided reading group and at the same time provide meaningful activities for the remainder of the class related to their literacy needs.

This book is written as a direct response to this difficulty in order to provide teachers with a management plan that enables them to work with each guided reading group in their classrooms while the remainder of the class works productively at "kidstations" where skills and concepts are reinforced. We call this approach the Guided Reading Kidstation Model, or the kidstation model, as we like to refer to it. The model can be described as flexible grouping of students based on needs or interests, usually in four groups as teachers initiate the process. Each group works on tasks at kidstations that have been presented either to the whole class or an individual guided reading group. To ensure teacher accountability, the tasks are based on the *Standards for the English Language Arts* (1996) as outlined by the International Reading Association (IRA) and the National Council of Teachers of English (NCTE). Student accountability is ensured as students present their completed work accomplished in their kidstation group to their classmates following a specific schedule.

Chapter Overviews

Chapter 1, "Evolution of the Kidstation Model," answers the question, What do I do with the rest of the class when I am conducting a guided reading group? An explanation of guided reading is explored in the balanced literacy program and its relationship to the kidstation model. We discuss our rationale for creating a kidstation model that addresses teachers' concerns by providing them with a plan to create uninterrupted and meaningful time to work with guided reading groups while the remainder of the class is involved in worthwhile activities that reinforce skills taught during guided reading. Finally, we share the conclusions from our study, which took place in inner-city school districts in grades 1 through 6.

In chapter 2, "The 'Guided' Exchange: Making Informed Decisions About Creating and Managing Flexible Groups," we use the term *guided* to emphasize and explain the exchange of information from student to teacher and teacher to student as informed decisions are made regarding the teaching and learning process. This reciprocal role of information exchange has a direct impact on grouping, as well as instruction. Because grouping is a vital component of guided reading, decisions about grouping must be made with consideration of many influencing factors. What procedures are necessary for teachers to pursue to determine the student's level of literacy functioning? What are the criteria for grouping, and what kinds of groups should teachers create? What factors influence a teacher's decision when determining a student's placement in a group, or the reading selections to be used, or when a student should move on to another group? How do teachers manage flexible grouping in their classrooms? What procedures should teachers use to monitor the student's progress, and how often should teachers and students engage in the "guided" exchange? We address these questions and many other grouping concerns in this chapter as teachers gather relevant data to implement guided reading effectively.

Chapter 3, "Guided Reading and the Creation of Kidstations," is based on the fundamental principle of a balanced literacy program—that is, integrating reading, writing, listening, speaking, and viewing. The chapter presents information on how to conduct the guided reading lesson and then focuses on the individual kidstations. Each kidstation reflects the thinking processes of Bloom's (1984) taxonomy of categorizing questions. Kidstation One provides teachers with ideas and strategies for developing students' skill knowledge for word recognition and literal comprehension and the knowledge and comprehension levels of Bloom's taxonomy. Activities at this kidstation focus on decoding skills, structural analysis, vocabulary, and grammar, as well as comprehension. Kidstation Two provides students with opportunities to develop the skills of inferring—that is, to read between the lines. By reading or listening to text, students are exposed to different genres and text structures and infer the author's purpose or interpret the author's point of view. Students learn to analyze and apply the knowledge of the text thus incorporating the higher levels of Bloom's taxonomy. Kidstation Three provides students with opportunities to elaborate, create, synthesize, and make evaluations with regard to the text. Students think beyond the text as they engage in activities that move them to persuade, explain, think creatively, and participate in problem solving. Finally, Kidstation Four allows teachers to see the various ways students can present what they have created and completed in their workstations as they present individually or in small groups. The presentation of work fosters student accountability and responsibility for the work assigned in the kidstations. In addition, there is a description of a behavior management program, which includes a depiction of the demonstration for the students of the expectations for work and behavior while using the kidstation, as well as the establishment of rules for respecting other students and the teacher during the literacy block.

Chapter 4, "Implementing the Kidstation Model," builds on the previous chapter, explaining the five-day implementation cycle for guided reading and participation at each of the kidstations. An example of a possible room design is included as a key aspect for the success of the kidstation model.

Chapter 5, "Adapting Basal Readers, Trade Books, Leveled Readers, and Content Area Textbooks to the Kidstation Model," outlines the flexibility that kidstations provide teachers. Teachers are able to select activities from basal reading series, trade books, leveled books, and textbooks to use with the kidstation model. A variety of enriching ideas can be gleaned in part or whole from the teacher's manual accompanying these materials. The chapter includes sample activities that illustrate the ease of adapting materials from these sources.

Chapter 6, "The Kidstation Model: Q & A," includes questions and responses based on our initial article about the kidstation model, "Student Accountability: Guided Reading Kidstations" (Guastello & Lenz, 2005). This article inspired many teachers to implement the model outlined in chapter 4. However, some teachers had practical questions that are worth sharing with other practitioners in the field. For this reason, we have designed this chapter as a Q & A "chat room" where teachers can benefit from questions from their peers.

The book is designed as a conversation with teachers. In addition, we use case studies and examples of teachers who have used the kidstation model to show its practicality. There are numerous ideas in the appendixes for material that can be adapted and created for the kidstation activities. Appendixes A through F include examples of literacy profiles, guided reading checklists, reading and learning inventories, sample planning sheets for grouping and instruction, activities for the kidstations, and evaluation forms for student presentations. In addition, Appendix G lists websites that can be used directly by students at the kidstations or for activities that teachers can modify for the kidstations.

We hope that you find this book helpful as you work with your guided reading groups and use the kidstation model.

Acknowledgments

We would like to acknowledge all the teachers and students who participated in the pilot study for our kidstation model and all the teachers who worked with us to implement the model so successfully. We are also grateful to those teachers who shared their concerns and their accomplishments with us.

CHAPTER 1

Evolution of the Kidstation Model

Mrs. Martin, a second-grade teacher, has just completed a series of in-service workshops designed to teach her and her colleagues how to implement guided reading into the district's balanced literacy program. Mrs. Martin observes the instructor working directly with children and even participates in the guided reading group discussion with the students. Like her colleagues, she is very enthusiastic about conducting guided reading groups with her students. The idea of working with students in small groups would enable her to challenge and support the students as they develop their literacy skills. But like many teachers, she asks the same question when attempting to implement guided reading in their classrooms: What do I do with the rest of the class when I am working with a guided reading group?

There Must Be a Way to Manage My Guided Reading Groups

This question is often asked by teachers in our graduate literacy courses and during staff development workshops in schools. Fran developed the kidstation model as a direct response to the challenge that the classroom management of guided reading and independent work groups poses for kindergarten through sixth-grade teachers. As a result of working on previous literacy studies and teacher and parent workshops, together we collaborated on designing activities for the kidstations and conducted the staff development. We address the problem of classroom management by providing a plan using four kidstations and a five-day cycle. The activities presented are based on the *Standards for the English*

Language Arts of the International Reading Association and the National Council of the Teachers of English (IRA & NCTE, 1996), which involve reading, writing, listening, and speaking. These activities help to increase student accountability and productivity.

Components of Guided Reading

Guided reading is only one of the major components of a balanced literacy program and one activity in a continuum of literacy instruction. Guided reading springs from read-alouds, where the children are read to by their teachers. Reading aloud to children enables them to internalize sentence structure and understand book concepts, develop a strong listening vocabulary, and gain a sense of story structure. Likewise, with modeled reading teachers can demonstrate effective oral skills. Moving on to shared reading, reading *with* children, teachers focus on direct instruction of literacy skills, such as before, during, and after reading strategies; teaching a myriad of word recognition skills; and developing reading vocabulary and comprehension skills.

It is during guided reading, reading *by* the children, that teachers support each child's development of effective literacy strategies for processing text at increasingly challenging levels of difficulty (Fountas & Pinnell, 2001). Guided reading provides a platform for assisting readers in processing meaning from a variety of texts with understanding and fluency (Whitehead, 2002).

Guided reading is an instructional approach that involves a teacher working with a small group of children who are similar in reading behaviors and the text level they are able to read with support. The ultimate goal of guided reading is to help students learn how to use literacy strategies successfully (Fountas & Pinnell, 1996) and to create independent readers who can formulate questions, consider possibilities and alternatives, make informed choices as they acquire meaning from text, and problem solve when they encounter difficulties with the text (LaMere & Lanning, 2000). According to Spiegel (1992), the overall purpose is for children to read for meaning at all times.

The successful guided reading program involves several steps: (1) determining the independent level of each student; (2) leveling the books in the classroom library; (3) arranging students in four flexible groups by ability, interest, or skill development; and (4) selecting a book for each group to read independently with

90–95% accuracy. Other issues that must be addressed by the teacher are rotating the guided reading groups (Villaume & Brabham, 2001); using task management boards; establishing clear expectations for work, behavior, and following directions; and establishing workstations for independent groups. In addition, we have found that preplanning in terms of teaching students about the kidstations and initially modeling the guided reading sessions creates an effective flow for instruction and implementation of the kidstation model.

A guided reading lesson can take many forms. The major concern is that it is designed to meet the needs of the students in the group (Morrow, 2005). In the guided reading lesson, the teacher incorporates many experiences, such as working with word recognition, vocabulary, and comprehension. These experiences help students with phonograms, syntactic and semantic cues, and writing (Reutzel, 1998–1999). Once the teacher selects the book, the teacher gives an introduction and an overview, as well as elicits students' prior knowledge. Students skim through the text for difficult words as the teacher lists the words. The teacher explains the vocabulary through context and picture clues. The purpose of the lesson is established and then students read silently. As the children read, the teacher asks individual students to read to her. She listens to each student and marks a progress chart. The teacher interacts with each student to determine comprehension and to assist if the student has a problem or a question. The teacher asks individual students questions about the text and engages the group in a final discussion about the book. Subsequently, these students may have to develop certain skills that the teacher observed as needing further reinforcement, which will be addressed in the kidstations that follow the guided reading session.

While Mrs. Martin, like many of the teachers in the workshop noted at the beginning of the chapter, understood the concept of guided reading and observed several sessions with students and teachers in other schools and at their training workshops, she still encountered many problems with planning and implementing guided reading and managing the rest of the class while engaged with the guided reading group. Another factor that presented her with a challenge was the amount of time spent with each guided reading group. For these reasons, we stress the principles of guided reading, which focus on the needs of the learner.

Principles of Guided Reading

The role of the learner is emphasized in the guided reading process. In the past the "readiness model" dominated reading instruction, and educators believed that children should not be taught to read until they were 6½ years old (Smith, 2002). However, in 1971, psycholinguist Frank Smith challenged this view. He believed that reading was not something that one was taught, but rather something that was learned from the practice of reading as guided by their teachers (Pearson, 2002). The student and the teacher work together using strategies to decode and comprehend text. The guided reading format is especially beneficial for struggling and at-risk readers (Short, Kane, & Peeling, 2000). Research reveals that it is effective for building fluency (Stahl & Kuhn, 2002), comprehension (Dymock, 1998), and to encourage independent silent reading (Worthy, Broaddus, & Ivey, 2001). Matthews (1966) concludes that the flexible groupings in guided reading allow for maximum achievement.

Guided reading was proven to be a valuable method of instruction using informational materials (Villaume & Brabham, 2001). The 2000 report of the National Reading Panel (National Institute of Child Health and Human Development [NICHD], 2000) confirmed these findings by reporting that guided reading had a strong positive effect on word recognition, fluency, and comprehension across a range of grade levels. The kidstation model incorporates activities that help to develop these aspects of literacy.

What Are the Components of the Kidstation Model?

The kidstation model is composed of four kidstations using a five-day cycle. Each kidstation addresses one of the first four English language arts standards (IRA & NCTE, 1996). Kidstation One focuses on Standard 1, which calls for students to use language for information and understanding. The activities in this kidstation help to develop word recognition, vocabulary, and literal comprehension. Kidstation Two calls for students to use language as a means for reading, writing, and responding to the wealth of literature and subject area content that is available. The activities in this kidstation incorporate the principle of Standard 2, responding to the literature. Kidstation Three emphasizes Standard 3, which calls for students to use language for critical analysis and evaluation. The activities in this kidstation challenge students to elaborate in response to the literature and develop the ability to think beyond the text.

Kidstation Four is really not a kidstation per se, but a presentation by each student in the group. Kidstation Four focuses on Standard 4, which calls for students to communicate effectively with a variety of audiences. In this kidstation, students have the opportunity to use language for social interaction and to talk about and share their learning experiences with their peers and then demonstrate what they created and learned. This is where the element of accountability is generated. At the end of a five-day cycle, each student in one group has the opportunity to demonstrate to the class what he or she has created or completed in the kidstation. Students are evaluated not only on the work they complete but also on their ability to present it to the class. (See chapter 4 for a more detailed explanation of each of the kidstations within the five-day cycle.)

A Model That Works: Sharing the Experiences

We developed and implemented the kidstation model in urban school districts in kindergarten through sixth grade in low socioeconomic areas in the South Bronx and Manhattan with a large percentage of children reading below grade level. The student population in each school ranged from 70–80% African American and from 20–30% Hispanic. The classes were overcrowded with as many as 30 or 35 students (Guastello & Lenz, 2005). Realizing that traditional centers would not be feasible in this setting, we created portable kidstations, or areas within the classroom where students could gather for guided reading and to complete assignments at different work areas.

After reviewing test scores and meeting with reading consultants from various publishing companies, the administrators in all of the districts decided to adopt a balanced reading program with heavy emphasis on guided reading. Funding for the program included provisions for teachers to attend workshops and training sessions and to observe teachers in other schools where guided reading was being used successfully. However, after two months of trying to implement the program, teachers encountered many logistical problems. We were invited to observe and interview teachers in several of the schools in the districts. Subsequently, we met with the teachers to listen to their concerns and share our observations.

Teachers' concerns revolved around the number of guided reading groups, students' behavioral issues, time spent on task, and the quality and completion of students' independent work while teachers worked with a guided reading group. In their large classes, these teachers felt stressed by having to work with several guided reading groups for 15 or 20 minutes each day. Teachers in the primary grades expressed concerns about having students working for sustained periods independently when they might be having difficulty with the tasks. Some primary- and intermediate-grade teachers spoke about how a few disruptive students often prevented their groups from working without being disturbed. Likewise, the students not in the guided reading group would often seek the teacher's assistance if they did not understand what they were supposed to be doing when the teacher was with the guided reading group. In addition, teachers were looking for ideas for independent work that would be meaningful for their students.

The model we developed is a synthesis of practical modifications that address teachers' concerns without compromising the principles of guided reading. We addressed each of their concerns and then demonstrated the kidstation model in their classrooms to enable them to see the benefits for them and their students. Some of the practical modifications addressed room design, establishing portable kidstations instead of centers, and increasing and being flexible with the time allotment for each guided reading group. Instead of the suggested 15 to 20 minutes with several guided reading groups in one day, teachers spent more time with one group as they initiated the kidstation model. We showed the teachers how to provide meaningful activities for their students while working with a guided reading group. (Samples of these activities are provided in chapters 4 and 5.) The students became observers during our demonstrations so that they could see the importance of working quietly and diligently while the teacher met with the guided reading group.

Teachers began to provide more quality time with each guided reading group as a result of using the kidstation model. They saw how essential it was to start out slowly and patiently

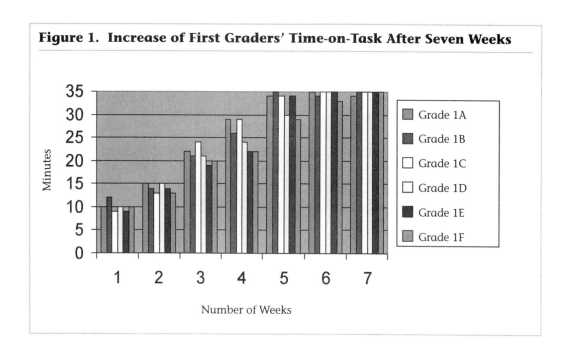

Figure 1. Increase of First Graders' Time-on-Task After Seven Weeks

and, more important, not to begin the guided reading process until appropriate planning had taken place. After three months of working with the teachers and students to implement the model, not only did students increase their time-on-task to the maximum of 35 minutes per session but they also increased the percentage of completed work. Figure 1 depicts six first-grade classes over a period of seven weeks. Each week an independent observer timed the students at work at the kidstations. By the seventh week, five out of six classes were working up to maximum time at the kidstations with a noted increase in time-on-task in each of the first four weeks.

Likewise, Figure 2 reports the percentage of completed work by the six classes of first-grade students at each of the kidstations as recorded by the teachers. As students began presenting their work, the percentage of completed quality work increased. This increase was maintained as students became comfortable with the presentation process.

The data on five fifth-grade classes is reported in Figure 3. The results indicate that students increased their time-on-task substantially by the third week and the maximum time from the fourth week through the duration of the school year. Figure 4 indicates the percentage of increased amount of completed

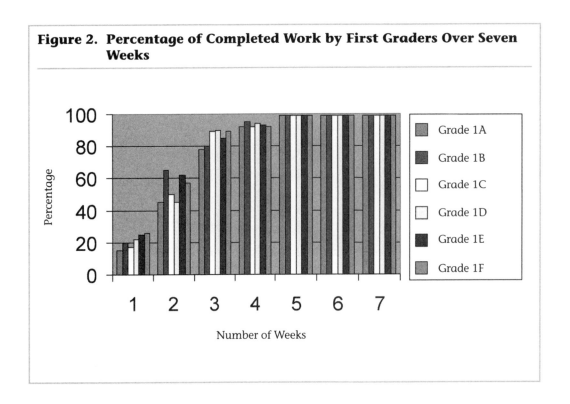

Figure 2. Percentage of Completed Work by First Graders Over Seven Weeks

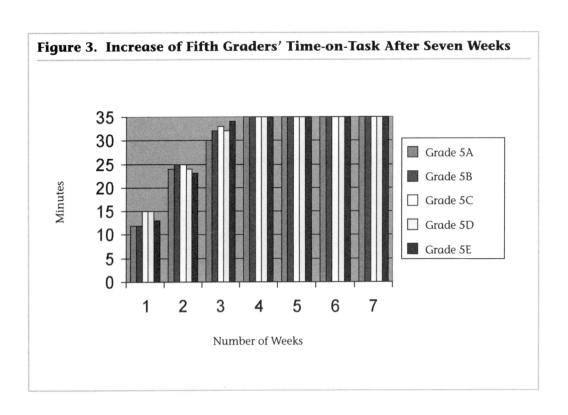

Figure 3. Increase of Fifth Graders' Time-on-Task After Seven Weeks

Figure 4. Percentage of Completed Work by Fifth Graders Over Seven Weeks

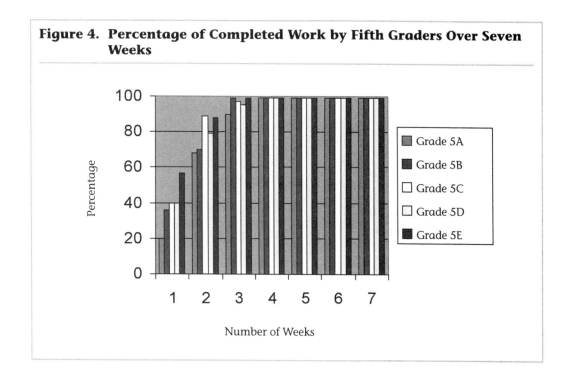

quality work as reported by each of the teachers. By the fourth week, the older students had achieved the expectations of the teachers in terms of completing their work independently in each of the kidstations.

Teachers reported that students were more interested in literacy activities as a result of the use of this model and they were more responsible about working well independently. They took greater pride in their work since there was more accountability during the presentation phase. Students looked forward to presenting their work. Teachers reported fewer behavior problems and more active listening since the implementation of this model. Furthermore, teachers indicated that there was more collaboration among grade-level teachers as they shared and prepared ideas for use in the kidstations. Overall, those teachers who used the kidstation model expressed satisfaction and enthusiasm with it.

In many cases, we also observed that English-language learners (ELLs) found the conversation, discussion, and demonstration aspects of the kidstation model to be helpful in learning not only the content but also the rhythm and patterns of the English language and how to use the language to express their ideas. By providing these students with opportunities to create their presentations, they were able to make the transition from social to academic language, a goal of Teachers of English to Speakers of Other Languages (TESOL, 1997). By using the kidstation model, teachers were able to meet the needs of the ELLs, as well as special needs students, more efficiently because specialists were able to collaborate with the classroom teachers on ideas for the kidstations. These specialists also "pushed-in" to the classrooms during guided reading time—that is, they became part of the teaching process by working specifically with the special needs students as the classroom teacher provided instruction to the remainder of the students. When time permitted, they were available to help ELLs and special needs students, as well as other students who were experiencing difficulty at kidstations.

In addition, the kidstations helped to accommodate the many different learning preferences found in classrooms, such as visual, auditory, and tactile or kinesthetic learners (see chapter 2 for more information on how the kidstations accommodate different learners). Finally, many ELLs, struggling readers, and special needs students also have difficulty with content area texts and the model can help with this by providing extensive use of visuals and hands-on materials as well as the teacher's support while reading (see chapter 5 for more information on adapting content area texts for these diverse learners).

In addition, with this model struggling readers and low achieving students are given direct instruction in areas of need in the context of their classroom. For example, students who were working on a poetry lesson and lacked decoding skills were shown in Kidstation One how to use manipulatives to develop the concept of onset and rime. At Kidstation Two, the students incorporated art in creating illustrations that depicted their understanding of cause and effect. Finally, at Kidstation Three the students used their imaginations to create a poem in which they reflected on the story they read.

Conclusion

The kidstation model answers many teachers' concerns for managing guided reading and independent work groups. The success of the model is documented in the improvement of students' reading scores, teacher and student attitude surveys, and an increase of collaborative efforts among teachers in two urban school districts. Behavioral issues decreased as student accountability increased. The best testimony comes from the teachers in the field. Mr. Sanchez, a third-grade teacher, notes,

> For me, the small guided reading groups enable me to really see my students' strengths as readers and where they need individual support. For my students, the model of the kidstations develops the standards and gives my students a reasonable amount of time to do their work independently and share what they have learned. I can readily say that from week to week I can see how much they have learned because of the opportunities they have at the kidstations to apply their knowledge.

How does a teacher acquire the necessary information about students to determine grouping and appropriate use of reading materials? Chapter 2 examines how teachers should begin the process.

The "Guided" Exchange: Making Informed Decisions About Creating and Managing Flexible Groups

Every classroom teacher is faced with several challenging realities no matter how many students are in the class. Whether there are 15 or 30 students, teachers know that there can be a wide range of knowledge base, language skills, and background experience among students. Furthermore, with the impetus for inclusion, the range of abilities, skills, and experience has become even more diverse. How does the teacher zero in on each student and determine his or her needs and what motivates each student to want to learn? How is the information communicated to teachers in order to make decisions about the teaching and learning process for each child? It is important that teachers realize that they, too, must be "guided" by information *about* their students and *from* their students to make informed decisions about how and what students must learn.

Guided reading takes place within the framework of small groups of five to seven students where a teacher listens to individual students as they read. While doing so, the teacher observes the reading behaviors of students to determine their needs and proficiencies as readers. But how are these groups determined? What "guides" teachers in the decision-making process as groups are determined and managed?

Let's Begin With Assessments!

Teachers need to gather data on each child before considering grouping. In fact, we highly recommended that teachers do not start the guided reading groups until the fifth or sixth week of school year. During those initial weeks in school, teachers must gather data on each student to determine his or her proficiencies and needs. Assessment is a powerful tool for identifying and addressing the specific needs of students (Shellard, 2003).

Periodic and systematic assessment is essential to "guide" teachers to make effective decisions. From examining schoolwide or districtwide tests and state test results to informal assessments, inventories, surveys, observations and notes taken during conferencing, teachers need to know what it is that their students know and what their students can do, with or without the teacher's assistance.

Assessment needs to be multidimensional, in that it should provide teachers with reliable and relevant information regarding a student's progress. Both formal and informal assessments are valuable tools in determining students' needs, learning preferences, and reading proficiencies. Running records, informal reading inventories, anecdotal recordings, writing samples, periodic criterion-referenced tests, observations, checklists, and notes from student–teacher conferences all provide teachers with pertinent data to redirect teaching and improve learning.

Assessment also needs to be dynamic, not just to measure what the student can do now, but it should also predict the student's potential for growth and change (Gunning, 2006). Dynamic assessment, based on Vygotsky's (1934/1978) view of how children learn (Haywood, Brown, & Wingenfield, 1990), holds that children learn higher order concepts through their interaction with peers and adults. As teachers observe students in the guided reading groups and interact with them, the information teachers share with students and students share with their teachers redirects the instructional process.

Developing Literacy Profiles

Teachers should consider creating a literacy profile for each student. Such a profile may contain inventories, which describe a student's personal interest and attitudes toward reading and writing. It may also have a checklist indicating the types of reading behaviors a student uses before, during, and after reading. The profile may have a description of a student's performance in terms of fluency, rate of reading, and phrasing. Also contained in the profile should be a list of books the students have read, as well as several writing pieces. Samples of two primary-grade and one intermediate-grade literacy profiles can be found in Appendix A. Table 1 also includes resources for additional samples of literacy profiles.

Running records and miscue analyses of each student's reading performance over time reveals the student's ability to use graphophonic, syntactic, and semantic cues and provides the teachers with information about the student's accuracy and self-correction. Sometimes teachers will audiotape their students to determine a more accurate assessment of fluency. Anecdotal records are another means of gathering information about a student, as well as using observations.

Informal reading inventories can often reveal a student's independent, instructional, or frustration levels, as well as their listening potential. Knowing what a student can do is an important starting point for the teacher in terms of selecting the appropriate level materials for the students to read. However, without overwhelming students with the burden of assessments, ongoing and periodic evaluations are necessary to guide teachers into making informed decisions to improve the teaching and learning process. Therefore, assessment should be an integral part of the teaching and learning process and be woven into daily routine practices. For example, using a simple checklist (see Appendix B), Mr. Maxwell listens to a student read aloud and notes what strategies a child uses or does not use when he or she encounters a problem when reading. Such observations immediately inform the teacher that a particular skill needs to be retaught, and this

---

Table 1. Resources for Literacy Profiles

Griffin, P., Smith, P.G., Ridge, N. (2001). *The literacy profiles in practice: Toward authentic assessment.* Portsmouth, NH: Heinemann. (ERIC Document Reproduction Service No. 458232)

Literacy profiles handbook: Assessing and reporting literacy development. (1990). Brewster, NY: Touchstone Applied Science Associates. (ERIC Document Reproduction Service No. 336715)

Many, J.E., Wallace, F.H., Stephenson, J., & Eickholdt, L. (2004, September/October). "I know them better than students in my on-campus courses": Exploring a personalized approach to online instruction. *Reading Online, 8*(2).

information obtained from the student "guides" the teacher to redirect instruction and improve the quality of teaching to enable the student to become proficient at that particular skill. While observing other students, Mr. Maxwell may discover there are several students who have a similar difficulty. Noting this, a teacher can make an informed decision as to how, when, and whom he or she must teach this skill and then a group is formed based on a skill need. The rationale for assessment lies in research on reading development that indicates the importance of basic skills for future success (Paris & Hoffman, 2004). Such information can also help teachers decide if students are benefiting from a particular program or an approach to reading and writing. It also identifies students who need extra resources and supportive interactions with teachers (Fountas & Pinnell, 2001) to ensure successful and effective learning. Another helpful tool is a Reading Behaviors Checklist (see Appendix B) to determine the strategies students use before, during, and after reading.

Interest inventories are also valuable tools for focusing on topics that will motivate students to read and write (see Appendix C). Such inventories, and those similar to them, tell students that their teacher genuinely cares about what interests them and how the students perceive themselves as readers and writers. A simple interest inventory can guide teachers to focus on specific areas of instruction using topics that students will explore and respond to when working in groups. A teacher might notice that a group of students are interested in finding out more about marine life. Through consultation with the school librarian, a teacher might ask to have these books available for his or her class during the school year and when reading about these topics in the guided reading groups and completing their follow-up activities in the kidstations.

Another area to explore with students is their learning preferences. Teachers need to know about differences in learning preferences of their students and adapt and accommodate, as much as possible, these differences as an expected part of their teaching responsibilities (Felder & Brent, 2005). For example, visual learners best receive information through seeing or viewing. They process information as it unfolds before their eyes. These students react to facial expressions and body language, and they use visualization to recall information from visual representations, such as pictures, graphs, charts, diagrams, transparencies, demonstrations, and movies. Knowing this, a teacher would not only give oral directions in class but also be mindful that these students (the visual learners) need to have written directions. They must see them to learn them (Burmark, 2002). These students would benefit form having class notes in front of them as the teacher speaks. This type of student finds it difficult to listen for a prolonged period of time. This information about how the students learn directs the teacher's creation of activities for the kidstation that address their learning preference. Such activities might include the use of transparencies, charts, diagrams, color, plays, and skits, and they could allow students time for drawing, sketching, designing, and viewing films.

In contrast, auditory learners process information from what they hear. These students can listen to lectures and like to engage in discussions and debates. They process meaning through the tone, pitch, and other nuances of someone's voice. Their activities might include listening to audiotapes, conducting interviews, story telling, reciting poetry, and participating in debates.

In addition, there are tactual, or kinesthetic, learners. They explore life through their sense of touch. These are the students who need to get up and move around and have frequent breaks when working. They exhibit good rhythmic movements, as well as fine and gross motor skills. They prefer hands-on learning, creating, demonstrating, learning by doing, manipulating materials, working on puzzles, and tracing. Activities for them at the kidstations should include drawing, painting, cutting, role playing, and constructing. Field trips are great for these students where teachers can follow up the experience with reading and writing activities.

There are many different learning preference and modality surveys available that can help teachers identify the types of learners sitting in your classroom, which will help with decisions regarding the kidstations activities. We have included our sample in Appendix C.

Having gathered initial data on the students, a teacher can develop the student literacy profile, which consists of information regarding the student's reading and writing activities, reading performance, attitude surveys, interest inventories, and other relevant information. With this student profile, the teacher is guided by the students to make informed decisions about the instruction.

As we know, whatever methods of assessment teachers choose to incorporate, errors can be made. Therefore, we recommend that

Table 2. List of Informal and Formal Assessments Used to Develop a Literacy Profile

Informal Assessments (Administered by the Teacher)	Formal Assessments (District- and Statewide Assessments)
Running Records	Terra Nova Achievement Test
Miscue Analysis	Iowa Test of Basic Skills
Interviews	English Language Arts Exam Grades 3–8
Phonics Mastery Test	Wide Range Achievement Tests
Dolch Basic Sight Words	Test for Auditory Discrimination
Informal Reading Inventory	
Early Literacy Profile	
Learning and Modality Preferences	
Reading Behaviors	
Interest Inventories	

teachers strive for a balance between standardized formal testing and holistic evaluations. Ongoing assessments, both formal and informal, enable both the teacher and student to monitor the student's progress. These periodic assessments should also indicate which of the strategies and resources have been employed to help each student. Opportunities for students to monitor their progress are highly beneficial and motivational. Periodically, teachers should be summarizing achievement and learning over a given period of time and sharing this information with both the students and their parents. Table 2 shows the different types of assessment that can be used to develop a literacy profile for students in your classrooms.

Students Guide Teachers: Making Decisions About Guided Reading Groups

While there are many factors that contribute to effective implementation of guided reading, one of the most important factors is decisions about grouping. Here is where "guided" becomes a reciprocal process. Teachers use information from students to guide their decision-making processes. This information includes students' responses to interest inventories, reading behavior checklists, and learning preference surveys (see Appendix B and C), as well as performance assessments.

One thing we as educators know for sure is that research advises against grouping solely by homogeneous ability (types of groups are discussed in more detail in the next section). In some cases, students are placed in a group according to their ability, and instead of progressing, they tend to digress (Ediger, 2000). Students in low ability groups tend to be bombarded with skill development only, with little opportunity for exploring topics of their interest or engaging in creative and challenging activities. Sometimes students tend to stagnate in these groups, which subsequently damages their self-confidence and self-esteem (Reutzel & Cooter, 2003). Furthermore, grouping students only on the basis of ability does not necessarily improve achievement (Fountas & Pinnell, 2001). The key is to incorporate different kinds of groups, concentrating on flexible or dynamic grouping. Flexible or dynamic grouping varies the types of groups and the students who participate in the groups. It prevents group stagnation and gives students with mixed abilities the opportunities to work together and capitalize on the commonalities and creativity.

To ensure successful learning in a positive learning environment, teachers must adhere to dynamic or flexible grouping, developing the ability to use many sources of student information to guide them as they assign students to groups. Teachers must keep in mind that grouping changes after assessments are made and that groups are formed for different purposes. Such considerations, "guided" by the students' performance and conferencing, will provide students with confidence as they progress on the road to becoming independent readers.

Types of Grouping

One type of grouping where students of varied ability reading levels can come together is in an interest-based group where students can be grouped heterogeneously. Using the information gathered earlier from the interest inventories, interest groups can be used when student explore topics through literature or other areas of interest. They are more likely to pursue a reading task and engage in the subsequent reading and writing related tasks.

Students may even attempt to read materials at a higher level (Gunning, 2006). For example, Mrs. Montero observed that the Harry Potter series by J.K. Rowling sparked a special interest in castles by a group of fifth graders. "Guided" by this information, Mrs. Montero capitalized on the opportunity to group these students and assigned them the story *Towers of Stone* by Joanne Mattern. Motivated by their interest in this topic, the teacher focused on how castles were used in different types of literature and developed the vocabulary related to this topic. When student were grouped by their interest, there was a tendency for everyone in the groups to contribute something, sharing what they knew about the topic. The teacher reported that the struggling readers felt comfortable and confident to engage in discussions. Even if the materials are difficult to read, a brief prereading introduction and discussion enables the struggling readers to comprehend the content because they are motivated by interest and they have some existing knowledge of the topic.

Another type of grouping might depend on the activities or projects that are involved after students have completed the reading of the text. Knowing that a number of students were proficient at using PowerPoint, the teacher assigned one group of students to create a PowerPoint presentation depicting the elements of fact and fantasy in the Native American folk tale "The Moon Cheese: A Tale From Mexico," retold by Jan M. Mike.

Still another type of grouping can be skill- or need-based grouping—that is, homogeneous groups. Teachers have the opportunity to observe students as they *prepare* to read, listen to them *as* they read, and confer with them *after* they read. Gunning (2006) refers to these as the before, during, and after reading behaviors. Again, using a reading behavior checklist, as previously mentioned, teachers can determine the types of reading behaviors the students need to develop. Observing such behaviors, teachers can determine which skills or strategies students use to read proficiently and which they do not use when they encounter a problem (Brown, 2004). After the students read the selection and engage in discussion with their teacher, he or she also can determine if the students are having difficulty with a specific skill and subsequently form a needs group to review a particular skill. For instance, when reading *How the Ocean Tides Came to Be*, a story retold by Virginia Driving Hawk Sneve, Mrs. Montero noted that some students were having difficulty determining cause and effect relationships. Although she initiated an on-the-spot discussion of cause and effect, Mrs. Montero knew she had to reteach this concept to a group of students who had difficulty understanding this concept. Subsequently, she was "guided" into forming a group of six students to engage in direct teaching of this skill using another story. She subsequently designed follow-up activities at the kidstations for this group to apply the skill they were taught. The skill-needs grouping is based on a teacher's knowledge of the skills students should know for their level, and it is a temporary group maintained for a brief period of instructional time (Schwartz, 2005).

Finally, one last type of grouping is by ability where teachers may decide periodically to challenge students with materials on or slightly above their reading level. In this instance teachers must make certain the appropriate reading materials are available for these groups. These are some ways that teachers can implement flexible grouping.

To incorporate flexible grouping that enables students to be challenged, it is helpful to use a planning sheet (see Appendix D, "Planning Sheet for Guided Reading Groups") that lists each child in a group with the books read and skills addressed and a second planning sheet (see Appendix D, "Planning Sheet for Guided Reading Activity") that determines the activities for the kidstations. Anecdotal comments about each child's ability to master the targeted skills provide the necessary information for establishing the next set of groups. This approach is especially beneficial in the primary grades where students make rapid progress from the emergent and early readers to transitional and fluent readers. Children can be moved easily to a group that reflects ever-changing ability.

Guided reading groups are generally changed monthly using the information from the planning sheet. Specific skills are reinforced in the kidstations. Evidence of the students' understanding is gathered from the work samples and also individual conferencing. The planning sheets should be designed to ensure that skills and strategies are developmentally appropriate for a specific reading stage. As an example for early readers, proficiency with strategies such as monitoring and self-correcting, noting spelling patterns, chunking words into phrases, and using pictures to extend understanding of text will provide a foundation for becoming transitional readers.

Teachers Guide Students: Forming Groups and Creating Kidstation Activities

Based on the data collected over the first weeks of school, teachers should begin to form initial guided reading groups within the sixth or seventh week of school year (maybe sooner for veteran teachers). Teachers often ask, "How many groups should I have?" When initiating guided reading groups for the first time, it is recommended that within a class of 25 to 30 students, there should be four groups. This will provide the teacher with a manageable framework, especially when starting this process. As previously mentioned, grouping must be flexible, not only in terms of who is in each group but also in the number of groups within a classroom. As teachers become familiar with the guided reading process and see the need for more groups or a different configuration of groups, they can make those adjustments, but as the process begins, we will focus on the four reading groups.

When students are assigned to groups, it is essential that teachers explain to the students why they have been assigned to a particular group and the purpose of the group. This explanation enables students to understand that their abilities, interests, and needs are being addressed in collaborative efforts to improve their literacy skills. If students know they are in a group to address a particular need shared by everyone in the group, students are more likely to ask questions, take risks to answer questions, and attempt to use strategies to overcome the difficulty (Ediger, 2000). They begin to realize that it is appropriate and expected of them to wonder, to think, to make mistakes, and to talk about their misunderstandings. Then the focus is not on whether they are right or wrong but that these experiences in the guided reading groups are part of the learning process. This grouping provides teachers with an avenue for assisting readers to process meaning from text with understanding and fluency (Whitehead, 2002). It allows for a context in which teachers continue to monitor and guide each reader's development of effective reading strategies at increasing levels of difficulty (Fountas & Pinnell, 2001). Teachers guide students to engage in daily opportunities to read, examine, respond to, and critically evaluate both narrative and expository text. One can see how the basic principles of guided reading are consistent with the constructivist views of learning. That is, teachers function as coaches guiding and questioning students about the strategies they use when they read and when they encounter reading difficulties (Hornsby, 2000).

The guided reading session begins as teachers give an overview of the story with a brief introduction and a purpose for reading. Teachers also guide the students to engage in prereading behaviors: From picture walks to reading charts, graphs, and captions, students are encouraged to think about what they already know about the topic or to relate the story to something they have previously read. Teachers may even ask students questions about the reading selection to activate their schema, calling on students to use their background experience to bring meaning to the text. With older students, teachers may call attention to key vocabulary words to be certain that students have an understanding of these words before reading the text independently.

Then, as the students in the groups begin reading independently, the teacher circulates among the group and asks each child to read aloud a portion of the text. The teacher listens to see if students are using the "during" reading strategies to obtain meaning and fluency. For example, while reading, Michael comes across the word *bit* in a story about caring for a horse. He asks his teacher, Mr. Rooney, "What is a bit? I thought the word *bit* meant like a little bit, a small amount." Here is where Mr. Rooney must make an instructional decision as a student attempts to read and understand the text (Schwartz, 2005). He decides to explain briefly how the word *bit* is used in this context and makes a note to inquire later in the discussion group to see if anyone else had difficulty with this concept. He also makes a note to determine if Michael understands what homographs are and how some words have multiple meanings. If other students in the group have the same difficulty as Michael, homographs could be part of the follow-up activities in the workstations following the guided reading discussions.

After the students have read the text independently, the group assembles for their discussion about the text based on the initial purpose of the grouping. The teacher guides the discussion based on questions the students may have had when he or she was listening to them read, guiding them to revisit their predictions, encouraging them to determine and understand the author's purpose, or prompting them to discuss their favorite part of the book.

Conclusion

In the guided exchange between teachers and students, teachers are constantly faced with making critical decisions that have an impact on instruction. Teachers must be mindful of always creating a climate that allows students to become part of a community of literacy learners. It is the quality of this exchange between the students and teachers that ultimately improves instruction and the students' reading performance. It is the result of appropriate and effective instruction that gives the students the support they need to continue to read and gain meaning from the text.

The guided exchange ensures that every child's needs are served. The quiet child who rarely speaks in class experiences greater comfort in the guided reading group because it is based on his or her developmental level, needs, or interests. Furthermore, the teacher has the opportunity to "listen in" and conference with the child to correct any difficulties with text or skills. This "special time" with the teacher builds an emotional connection.

Time spent in those first weeks of school assessing the child's literacy abilities, needs, and interests now provides the teacher with information needed to begin the guided reading groups. As chapter 3 unfolds, we will focus on the guided reading process and the creation of the kidstations, including conducting the guided reading session, preparing students to read, and creating and modeling the kidstation model effectively.

Guided Reading and the Creation of Kidstations

Guided by the data collected in the literary profile, teachers form the initial groups and are ready to begin the guided reading process. By this time, teachers are aware of their students' needs and have selected the appropriate materials for students to read according to the type of group (i.e., interest, needs, or ability). However, before presenting detailed information on the guided reading process, we would like to offer a few suggestions based on our experience that will enable teachers to initiate the process effectively. Conducting the guided reading session and also managing the rest of the class is a learning experience for teachers, as well as for students. First, it is important to consider the time element when planning guided reading sessions. Fountas and Pinnell (2001) suggest that each guided reading session last 15–20 minutes and that teachers meet with two to three groups a day. On a practical note, we suggest that teachers meet with one group for 30–35 minutes and meet one group each day. Teachers should proceed slowly until they are comfortable with the process and can manage the rest of the class and the kidstations simultaneously.

Another suggestion for teachers that we would like to emphasize is modeling the guided reading session with the first group while the other students observe. Research shows the effectiveness of teacher modeling (Ceprano & Garan, 1998; Mohr, 1998). Students need to understand what "guided reading" means, and more important, they need to know the purpose and function of each group. An effective way to "manage" the students is allowing and helping them to discover their role and the teacher's role in the guided reading group.

Conducting the Guided Reading Lesson

According to Fountas and Pinnell (2001), an effective framework for implementing the guided reading lesson includes the following steps:

1. The teacher selects the text.

2. As part of the prereading process, the teacher introduces the text and highlights processing strategies such as cause and effect, identifying the main idea, using inference skills, and so forth.

3. Students read the text independently.

4. As part of the postreading process, the students and teacher discuss and revisit the text.

The following sections illustrate how Mrs. Walmar implements this process.

Prereading: Getting Students Ready to Read

Research has shown that having students engage in prereading activities, such as previewing the story, explaining the purpose of the story, and acquainting students with skills they will need to comprehend the text greatly increases the students' ability to understand and make inferences as they read (Roe, Smith, & Burns, 2005). Other prereading activities are designed to arouse students' interest, activate their prior knowledge, enable them to make predictions, and clarify vocabulary (Tierney & Readence, 2004). Prereading activities for guided reading also may include introducing key vocabulary words to ensure students understand their meaning. If the text had captions, charts, or graphs, the teacher also may direct the students' attention to facilitate understanding or, while skimming through the text, prompt students to ask questions regarding the text features or unfamiliar words.

Mrs. Walmar arranges the guided reading group in the center of the classroom. The remaining students are seated in a circle around the group. She explains to the entire class that this group is going to read a short story selected from a set of guided readers. Mrs. Walmar further explains that the students will engage in a discussion about the short story after they read the text independently. She also explains that she created this group based on the students' need to develop the skill of identifying cause and effect.

Before she continues, she turns to the students watching the lesson and instructs them to write down what they observe her and their classmates doing during this demonstration lesson. The students listen attentively as Mrs. Walmar continues the lesson. Addressing the students in the guided reading group, she gives a brief demonstration of cause and effect. She blows up a balloon and asks the students what causes the balloon to inflate. The students articulate that blowing the air into the balloon is the cause and that the balloon becoming larger is the effect. Further, they indicate that there would not be an effect (a large balloon) if there were no cause (blowing air into the balloon). Likewise, some events in a story are the result (effect) of something that happens (cause).

After distributing the text to each of the students in the guided reading group, the students listen as Mrs. Walmar gives a brief introduction to the text. Giving them this introduction enables students to get the gist of the story and can provide for fluent reading (Clay, 1993).

After showing them the text they are about to read, Mrs. Walmar explains that one of the characters in the story is moving to a new place. Some events in the story will cause Katie (the main character) to be unhappy and some events will cause her to change her feelings.

> **Mrs. Walmar:** As you read to yourself, remember how we talked about cause and effect. That's what we will discuss after you have read the story.
>
> **Jason:** So like with the example of the balloon, the cause makes the effect happen.
>
> **Mrs. Walmar:** That's correct, Jason. Your goal is to find the cause-and-effect events in the story. That is our main purpose for reading today.

Likewise, as part of the prereading process, Mrs. Walmar asks the students to make predictions, which she writes down on chart paper. They will revisit these predictions after they read the story.

Students Read Independently: Teacher Listens

A critical aspect of guided reading is when the teacher listens to each student read aloud. The students' oral reading and answers to the teacher's questions are vital for making informed decisions regarding instruction for each student (Fountas & Pinnell, 2001). Figure 5 shows a teacher listening as a student pauses to think through a difficulty he has encountered. The teacher is there to offer assistance and to make note of if and how the student remedies the problem. In fact, research shows that students who interact with their teacher and are supported by them during reading related activities tend to extend and enrich their learning in the process (Antonacci, 2000).

As the students in her guided reading group begin to read, Mrs. Walmar sits next to each student and asks him or her to read aloud to her. As each student reads aloud, Mrs. Walmar makes a note on the checklist on her clipboard. Mrs. Walmar may use such notations to indicate that a student read fluently, that a student had to reread a passage to clarify the meaning, or that a student did not understand a phrase containing figurative language. Ryan, the next student she approaches, stops reading and asks Mrs. Walmar a question. While reading the story *The Wild West* by Mika-Lynn Sokoloff, Ryan asks, "Mrs. Walmar, why do they keep the campfire burning all night on the ranch?" Mrs. Walmar responds with another question, which triggers a response from

Figure 5. Teacher Provides Support to Student Reading Independently

Ryan: "Well, Ryan, let's think about the setting of the story, the title of story, and look carefully at the picture. What are some reasons why they might need the fire at night?" Ryan thinks for a moment and realizes that they are out in the *wild* west in the desert. He responds by saying that they probably need the fire to keep away the *wild* animals, and they need it for light and heat. Mrs. Walmar notes that Ryan uses his schema of the west and his understanding of the word *wild* to make inferences and then continues to list reading behaviors as some students attempt to "think and talk through" the difficulties they encounter while reading. She listens and watches how Ramon looks at pictures first before he reads the page and how he makes use of context clues when he encounters an unfamiliar word. The students in the observation circle watch as Mrs. Walmar provides needed support to enable the students to read independently and fluently.

The information Mrs. Walmar gathers as she interacts with the group will help her to determine the kinds of activities students will explore in the kidstations. At some point, she may need to confer with the student who she observed reading and rereading a page in the text. Conferring with the student at a time when she sees that he or she is struggling has a positive impact on the student's determination and motivation to continue to read (Anderson, 2000). Through assisting the student in removing or explaining the obstacle, the teacher can allow the student to apply more cognitive energy on comprehending the story. After Mrs. Walmar listens to each child in the group, she waits until the group finishes reading.

Postreading: Time for Discussion

Postreading discussion takes place after each child in the group finishes reading the text. During the discussion, the students review their predictions and the teacher determines how well the students have fulfilled their purpose for reading the story (Fountas & Pinnell, 2001).

It is not uncommon for students to reread the text during guided reading, particularly in the lower grades. However, when the students complete the reading, Mrs. Walmar invites them to participate in a discussion where connections will be made between students' life experiences and the text. As previously mentioned, the focus for this lesson is to determine the cause and effect events in the story. While engaging the students in thoughtful conversation regarding the text, Mrs. Walmar is deliberate in her questioning strategies, which extend across the literal, inferential, critical, and creative levels of thinking. This discussion lasts approximately 12 minutes as each student in the group gives examples of how cause and effect events are established in the story.

Kayla remarks that she once felt like the girl in the story when she first moved into the neighborhood and had to start a new school.

Luis: What did you do to fit in?

Kayla: Nothing at first, then I joined the girls' basketball team and made friends with my teammates. After that, it was easier for me to make new friends.

Mrs. Walmar listens and realizes that writing about Kayla's experiences could be part of the follow-up at Kidstation Three with activities where Kayla and the other students can creatively elaborate on this topic.

Mrs. Walmar, guided by the notes on the clipboard, encourages the students to reflect on the problems they encountered while reading, noting strategies they used while reading and how they might apply these strategies to help them read other books.

Managing the Rest of the Class

As previously mentioned, an important part of managing the class involves modeling the first guided reading session for the entire class. Through modeling, the teacher is able to establish a framework for effective management because students are better able to grasp their responsibilities. For example, Mrs. Walmar instructs the students who are not directly involved in the guided reading session to observe her and their classmates and make note of the procedures, interactions, and behaviors as she conducted the session. After the session, she addresses the students who observe the lesson (that is, those students not in the guided reading group).

Mrs. Walmar: Well, who can tell me what I did during this lesson?

Michael:	You explained to the students why they were part of a group and then you spoke a little bit about the story.
Mrs. Walmar:	Very good, Michael.
Marsha:	You sat next to each of them and listened to them read out loud.
Jamal:	You helped Rosa answer her own question by asking her another question.
Mrs. Walmar:	That's right, and did you see how she thought a little more about her answer? She really did know the answer.
Jim:	I watched you write notes on your clipboard, Mrs. Walmar. Was that because you wanted to ask questions later?
Mrs. Walmar:	That's right and I really appreciated the fact that it was quiet enough for me to write down my comments as I listened to everyone read.
Oscar:	After the group finished reading, you asked questions about the causes and effects that took place in the story.
Daina:	And all the students in the group answered the questions you asked.

Then Mrs. Walmar asks the students why it is possible for her to listen to each student read and assist them. The students realize that the room needed to be at a "low buzz" in order for their teacher to hear the students read aloud and for the students to be able to read without any disturbance. Samuel notes that no one came up to the teacher to ask a question while she worked with the students in the group. It is important for all the students to realize that certain classroom protocol is necessary in order for Mrs. Walmar and their classmates in the guided reading group to carry out their responsibilities. Thus, Mrs. Walmar and the students recognize the need to create classroom courtesy tips for times when the students and their teacher are engaged in the guided reading group. Mrs. Walmar ensures that all the students realize that they will each have the opportunity to work with their teacher and will be given her individual attention.

We recommend creating a simple list of classroom courtesy tips with the help of the students. The chart may include items such as the following:

- Everyone in my class is entitled to learn.
- I need to be respectful of my teacher and classmates when they are working in the guided reading group.
- When my teacher is working with the guided reading group, I should not interrupt my teacher or my classmates.
- I need to use my time to complete my work.
- I should return all materials to the kidstations when I am finished.

By creating the chart, students are able to better understand such things as the importance of the teacher hearing students read, the need to keep their voices down in class and, once they are familiar with the kidstation activities, the importance of not getting up and asking the teacher for help. The students learn to use their group members as resources, as well as the sample of the work and directions readily available at their kidstation.

Types of Kidstations

Traditionally, centers are permanent physical locations in a classroom designed for a specific purpose (Isbell & Exelby, 2001). These centers provide students with a specific purpose, equipment, and materials to work with independently on a given task. For instance, one center could have several sets of headphones where students can listen to a taped story, or another center may have computers where students can develop their writing skills or research information on the Internet. In any given classroom, there can be many types of centers that support curricula goals: art centers, science centers, writing centers, and many more (Ford & Optiz, 2002).

However, the concept of permanent centers in most inner-city crowded classrooms is not a reality. Over the years of working in large-size classes, we have established the portable center or "kidstation." The term *kidstation* also affords students a sense of ownership because it is their special place to do their work.

The three types of kidstations we recommend support the tenets of the *Standards for the English Language Arts* (IRA & NCTE, 1996) and the components of reading as identified by the National Reading Council Committee on Preventing Reading Difficulties in Young Children (Snow, Burns, & Griffin, 1998). These components of phonemic awareness, phonics instruction, word recognition, fluency, vocabulary development, and comprehension instruction are considered essential in the acquisition of reading behaviors that allow students to become independent readers. Furthermore, the language arts processes of reading, writing, listening, speaking, and viewing are integrated into the literacy activities of the kidstations. The unique quality of the kidstation model is the concept of developing oral language (speaking) for communication through presentation. This aspect of the model is paramount in building in and maintaining the element of student accountability.

In addition, the kidstations help to accommodate students' different learning styles—that is, their approaches to or ways of learning. As previously mentioned, different types of learners include visual, auditory, and tactile or kinesthetic learners. Visual learners prefer to learn through seeing or viewing; they may think in pictures and learn best from visual displays, including diagrams, illustrated textbooks, overhead transparencies, videos, and handouts. Auditory learners prefer to learn by listening. These learners benefit from reading aloud and listening to tape recorders. Tactile or kinesthetic learners learn best through a hands-on approach involving moving, doing, and touching (Felder & Brent, 2005). To appeal to all students in the classroom, including English-language learners and special needs learners, the kidstations need to incorporate all of these learning modalities (Churchill, Durdel, & Kenney, 1998).

Preplanning for Kidstation Activities

As previously mentioned, teachers should use the first weeks of school to

- assess students' literacy performance;
- create a literacy profile on each student complete with inventories and surveys;
- teach the students different literacy activities that they will encounter later on in the kidstations;

- teach, demonstrate, and model presentation skills;

- use one group to model the guided reading process while other students observe the teacher and students interacting in the grouping; and

- create the classroom courtesy tips together with the students for working with the teacher in the guided reading group and working independently at the kidstations.

In addition, similar to the idea of formulating groups, creating the kidstations involves preliminary planning at the beginning of the school year. During the first month of school, teachers use the stories from basal readers, trade books, anthologies, and content area subject matter to demonstrate a variety of literacy activities that students will re-create at the kidstations. It is important for teachers to engage in preplanning for the kidstations during the first weeks of school when they can build a quality foundation for the guided reading process and the subsequent work at the kidstations (Perlmutter & Burrell, 2001). For instance, after reading a segment of one of the books in the Harry Potter series, we taught all the students how to make a vocabulary quilt as a means of learning how to use a thesaurus and apply their understanding of new vocabulary words (see Appendix E for directions on making a vocabulary quilt). Each student received a written set of directions, and we showed the students how to read and interpret the directions as we guided them through the process of making a quilt. Figure 6 shows a bulletin board displaying the students' vocabulary quilt. Later, students can use the bulletin board as a resource area when learning new vocabulary.

Over time, students learn several activities for enriching their reading and writing experiences (see chapter 5 for additional activities and Appendix G for websites that can be used directly by students at the kidstations or for activities that teachers can modify for the kidstations). By explicitly teaching students to manage the kidstation tasks, teachers help student create procedures and organizational strategies that encourage and enable students to function independently (Perlmutter & Burrell, 2001). By the time teachers are ready to start the kidstations, the students have learned several activities that they can work on independently without having to interrupt their teacher to ask for directions. This

Figure 6. Vocabulary Quilt

is important in terms of classroom management and student accountability.

Another aspect of conducting the guided reading discussions and creating the kidstations activities is incorporating effective questioning strategies. We believe that in order for teachers to develop such questioning strategies, they should be familiar with Bloom's taxonomy of categorizing questions (Bloom, 1984). The categories include knowledge, comprehension, application, analysis, synthesis, and evaluation. Teachers develop the appropriate types of questions to emphasize in conjunction with the focus of each kidstation For example, in Kidstation One, the focus is on incorporating knowledge- and comprehension-type questions or directives: Students are asked to define, label, list, classify, describe, and discuss. In Kidstation Two, the focus is on application and analysis: Students are asked to demonstrate, illustrate, and dramatize and to compare, diagram, and relate. In Kidstation Three, the focus is on synthesis and evaluation: Students are asked to create, design, and revise and to appraise, justify, and defend.

To help teachers plan for the guided reading kidstation activities, we designed a planning sheet (see Appendix D, "Planning Sheet for Guided Reading Groups"). The planning sheet serves as an organizational tool for the teacher and indicates the members of a particular guided reading group, the text used, skills and strategies to be reviewed, and the activities for each of the kidstations. Teachers determine the activities for the kidstations after they have listened to and observed the guided reading group. In addition, the activities in the kidstations can be shared by many teachers so that, over time, teachers have a variety of activities to tailor and use with their students. This is especially true in schools where there is more than one class on a grade level.

Kidstation One: Word Study and Literal Comprehension

The focus of Kidstation One is on word recognition, obtaining knowledge, vocabulary development, and literal comprehension. It addresses the first English language arts standard, which calls for students to use language for information and understanding (IRA & NCTE, 1996). As listeners, viewers, and readers, students collect data, facts, and details. They discover relationships, concepts, and generalizations and learn to use knowledge generated from oral, written, and electronic sources. As speakers and writers, students learn to use words effectively to express their ideas clearly and vividly, following the conventions of the English language to acquire, apply, and transmit information.

The first guided reading kidstation focuses on word recognition skills, which enhance reading fluency (Simpson & Smith, 2002). For example, in the primary grades, Mr. Henry reads his first graders *Which Is Which?* by Sharon Fear. As part of their word study activity, the children are given a slider on which to practice the family words for ___ig (see Appendix E for directions for this activity). By manipulating the slider, the students are able to form the words *big*, *dig*, *fig*, *pig*, *twig*, and *wig*. Then each student finds the matching pictures that are provided on a worksheet. The students match the word with the picture and then use each of the new words in a sentence.

While listening to a third-grade student read, Mr. Maxwell notes that several students had difficulty reading two-syllable words ending in a consonant–*le* pattern. The students do not know if the vowel in the middle was long or short. For example, Jason keeps encoding the word *bugle* as /bug–le/ and the word *rifle* as /rif–le/. The next day, at Kidstation One, the teacher arranges for students to listen to a number of words that contain the consonant–*le* pattern. They have to determine if the vowel in the first syllable is long or short. After listening to the words and determining which category the word belongs in, the students discover the pattern in the words. If the word has a short vowel sound, the first syllable has a consonant–vowel–consonant pattern (CVC) as in the word *humble*. If it has a long vowel sound as in the word *bugle*, the first syllable of the word has a consonant–vowel pattern (CV) before the consonant–*le* pattern. Once the students discover the pattern, they are able to read an additional 20 words with the consonant–*le* pattern fluently. Subsequently, they write a poem with the words ending in consonant–*le* pattern, which they read to the class on their presentation day. This is the work they are accountable for producing and asked to present as part of the five-day cycle.

While listening to students in another guided reading group, Mr. Maxwell notes that some students had difficulty with compound words, inflectional endings, and syllabication of multisyllable words. For Kidstation One, the teacher creates a Seek and Find activity, which helps to reinforce the learning of word parts, new vocabulary, and grammar elements. For example, in this case, the word learning for the activity is based on the book *Ice Walk* by Cass Hollander (see Appendix E for this activity, which can be adapted to different stories). Students must seek and find five contractions in the story and write out the two words that make the contractions, or they must use a thesaurus to seek and find synonyms for the key vocabulary words for this story.

Kidstation One also provides students with activities that improve vocabulary development through the use of context clues, analogies, word origins, synonyms, antonyms, homographs, homophones, and classification skills, just to name a few. For example, when fourth-grade students read about marine biology in science class, the teacher designed a word study activity (see Appendix E, "Word Origin") to help students learn that the word part "ology" means "study of...," and as they made the word puzzle, they learned of other sciences in which the same the word part is used (e.g., zoology). After the activity, one student wrote about seismology, a topic he wished to further explore. Figure 7 shows a student completing a word origin puzzle and,

Figure 7. Student Completing Word Origin Puzzle

thus, learning about the meaning of words containing the word origin *phobia*.

Another activity in Kidstation One focuses on word meaning. For example, fourth-grade students learned in their language arts class to use a thesaurus to find synonyms and antonyms for key words. Then they each made vocabulary jumpers, which they displayed on the bulletin word. A vocabulary jumper is a manipulative used to show synonyms and antonyms for a key word. The key word is listed at the top on the note card and accordion-like paper strips are attached to it. Synonyms are listed on the front of the strips and antonyms are listed on the back. The students shown in Figure 8 are selecting the vocabulary jumpers from the board that they wish to use as they revise their writing pieces.

Kidstation One also provides students with the opportunity to improve their literal comprehension. After students read *The River Rescue* by B.G. Hennessy, they are given a list of events intentionally arranged out of order. They have to cut up these sentence strips and arrange them in the proper sequence in the story (see Figure 9). When the task is complete, they use the

Figure 8. Students Choosing Vocabulary Jumpers

sequence or transition words from their writers' craft toolkits to rewrite the story summary using appropriate sequence connectors. The writer's craft toolkit is a notebook where students generate ideas for writing and compile lists of words to use with specific types of writing. For example, a student refers to their list of transition words when writing directions, explaining how to do something, or retelling a story in the proper order. When students complete their work at the kidstation, they place it in a box for the teacher to check, respond to, and provide positive feedback.

Other activities for Kidstation One that focus on literal comprehension and word study include creating K-W-L charts (Ogle 1986), which detail what students Know, what they Want to learn, and what they have Learned; activities for gathering information, such as using a thesaurus to expand word knowledge; using semantic maps to describe characters in a story or to summarize stories; and using the computer to design book jackets, brochures, PowerPoint presentations, and charts depicting data about information they have acquired. For example, the teacher in Figure 10 is explaining to a group of second graders

Figure 9. Sequencing Activity for *The River Rescue*

Directions: Paco is having a difficult time telling friend Jacob about the story *The River Rescue*. He seems to have mixed up all the events in the story. Can you help him retell the story in the correct order? Cut up each sentence and place them in the correct order. Then write a story summary using your "sequence connectors" to retell the story.

> The children had their breakfast and packed the car with their toys.

> The tubes and the raft with their lunch floated down the river.

> Roberto and Rosa were stranded on the island.

> Mother greeted them when they returned home that night.

> Father had to rescue Roberto and Rosa from the island.

> One Saturday morning, Dad decided to take Roberto and Rosa on a picnic at the river.

> The river policeman came to shore bringing Roberto and Rosa their raft with their lunch.

> Roberto was the navigator on the trip helping dad with directions to the river.

> Rosa went fishing and Roberto made sand castles.

> Dad set up the picnic blanket and watched Roberto and Rosa as they played.

> The river was too deep for Roberto and Rosa to swim across.

> Rosa and Roberto floated on their tubes over to the island to play.

how to use the story grammar wheel when determining the elements of a story. As they identify the elements of the story, they write it down on the Story Grammar Wheel Base (see Appendix E, "Story Grammar Wheel Base and Overlay"). The students will use this wheel as a graphic organizer in a prewriting activity that will support their construction of a story summary. The student shown in Figure 11 is using the Story Grammar Wheel to guide her as she writes her story summary.

Figure 10. Teacher Explaining How to Use Story Grammar Wheel

Figure 11. Student Using Story Grammar Wheel

Kidstation Two: Responding to the Literature

The second English language arts standard, which calls for students to use language as a means of reading, writing, and responding to the literature (IRA & NCTE, 1996), is addressed in activities in Kidstation Two. This standard requires that students listen to or read oral, written, and electronically produced texts; relate the material to their lives; and develop an understanding of the diverse social, historical, and cultural dimensions the text represents. Students are expected to comprehend, interpret, and critique imaginative text in every medium. The activities in Kidstation Two are designed to engage students in a deeper understanding of a text by drawing conclusions, determining the main idea, and understanding cause and effect relationships. Figure 12 shows a second-grade student using the cause and effect board to demonstrate her ability to link cause and effect relationships in a story.

In Kidstation Two, students have opportunities to read or listen to different genres, learn different text structures, infer the

Figure 12. Student Using Cause and Effect Board

author's purpose, interpret the author's point of view, and relate texts or performances to their own lives. The activities designed for this kidstation focus on developing the reader's ability to "read between the lines" using inferential skills.

As speakers and writers, students learn to use oral and written language for self-expression. This standard also requires that students present interpretations, conduct analyses, and synthesize reactions to the content and language of the text. Furthermore, it involves producing imaginative texts.

For example, Mr. Henry's first graders put the events from the short story in the correct sequence using a series of picture cards made from the story. After they arrange the pictures in order, they write a sentence under each picture to explain what occurred in the story. These sentences are later used in a story summary.

Mrs. Walmar's group, who read and previously discussed the concept of cause and effect in their guided reading group, have the chance to read another story and determine the cause and effect relationship on their own as part of an activity in Kidstation Two. After reading *The Lesson*, a two-act play by Judy Mayer, the children used a cause and effect board to demonstrate that they can determine the cause and effect relationship in the play.

The activities in Kidstation Two involve expanding students' vocabulary and switching genres. Samantha, a student in Mrs. Walmar's class, enjoyed reading *Head First* by Mike Dion. The main character in the story works very hard at overcoming her fear of learning how to dive head first. Samantha interpreted this story and wrote a poem (see Figure 13), based on a variation of Lee Bennett Hopkins's list poems, to illustrate her interpretation of how the main character in the story overcomes her fear. Samantha also wrote a short story about herself revealing how she overcame her fear of riding a bicycle without training wheels.

Older students may be expected to synthesize, interpret, and make connections based on what they've read or heard. Many times, older students engage in writing their autobiographies— some students even download music and pictures from the Internet to enhance their computer-generated presentations. With today's technology, students are capable of scanning their baby pictures and other photos from the past and integrating them into their electronic autobiographies.

In Kidstation Two, activities are designed to allow students to respond to the text. An activity may require the students to interpret the author's point of view and then react to the author by

---

Figure 13. Student Poem: Diving, Head First

Diving, Head First

By Marsha

Diving high,
Diving low,
Diving belly-flop,
Diving, oh no!

Diving opponent,
Diving champ,
Diving board,
Diving ramp.

Diving confident,
Diving scared,
Diving deep,
Diving weird!

Diving championship,
Diving meet
Diving head first,
Diving feet!

---

writing their own point of view on the topic. They can pretend to be a historical character and rewrite an event in history from their perspective or write letters to their classmates about the character's life. Older students can be given opportunities to recognize and react to stylistic, structural, and linguistic factors of different genres.

Kidstation Three: Elaboration

Kidstation Three provides students with opportunities to develop the third English language arts standard, which calls for students to use language for critical analysis and evaluation (IRA & NCTE, 1996). It challenges students to go beyond the text. As listeners, readers, and viewers, students are expected to analyze and evaluate experiences, ideas, information, and issues using critical thinking and evaluation criteria from a variety of perspectives. They must learn to formulate opinions and support those opinions by interpreting informational and persuasive texts, such as ads, commercials, or letters to the editors. Students learn to differentiate between fact and opinion, make decisions about the logic and believability of the text, and consider the appeal of characters in a picture.

At Kidstation Three, Mr. Henry's first graders, after having read *Which Is Which?* are asked to create five different ways that the mother pig could tell her piglets apart. They can draw a picture and write a sentence that gives the reader an explanation of how the problem is solved.

Reading different versions of fairy tales or legends, an activity at Kidstation Three, might require that the students recognize and write about the similarities and differences. Students elaborate on the themes or ideas expressed in various types of genres. After reading *The Mystery of the Gold Pen* by Nat Gabriel, students in a fifth-grade class are asked to make a personal reflection about how they would feel in a similar situation and to use their problem-solving skills to determine alternate solutions to the mystery of the missing pen. The activity challenges them to read beyond the words and create an alternate ending of the story (see Figure 14). For example, some students use their computer skills to write and illustrate an alternate ending to a story and present it as a PowerPoint presentation.

Another activity students can complete is to write about the story from Ms. Harmony's perspective and examine how she may have felt being accused of stealing the pen. In Kidstation Three, students explore their creativity and elaborate on ideas they have read.

Figure 14. Making a Personal Reflection: *The Mystery of the Gold Pen*

Can you image being Ms. Harmony accused of stealing a pen from Mr. Torp? Ms. Harmony is very upset to know that all the teachers and students in the school are buzzing about her stealing Mr. Torp's gold pen.

How would you feel if you were Ms. Harmony?
I think I would feel really bad that other people thought I stole the pen. I would feel like they couldn't trust me. Maybe I wouldn't want to work there anymore.

What could have been some solutions to the problem of the missing pen?
Maybe Mr. Torp left it in the library when he took his class there. One of his students could have borrowed the pen and left it in the library. It could have fallen out of his pocket and someone picked it up and put it on Ms. Harmony's desk. He could have asked her if she took it rather than making others think she did.

Kidstation Four: Presentations

Kidstation Four, which is really not a kidstation but the presentation stage, incorporates the fourth English language arts standard, which calls for students to use language for social interaction and presentation (IRA & NCTE, 1996). This standard requires that students learn to use oral communication in formal and informal settings with a wide variety of audiences. Learning to address different audiences reflects how students communicate in different situations. As readers, writers, and speakers, students are expected to learn how to use oral language, visuals aids, and technology to communicate ideas and enhance personal relationships with others.

From show-and-tell–type activities in the primary grades to sophisticated PowerPoint presentations in the middle and upper grades, students learn how to present the activities created at the kidstations to various audiences. At the end of a five-day cycle, the individual students in *one* of the guided reading groups will make a presentation of their work to designated audiences.

This is where the element of student accountability is evident. Students now learn that the work they are doing in the kidstations is not "busy work." It is a task that must be completed and eventually presented to an audience.

In the primary grades, it can be the retelling of a story or an explanation and demonstration of how to make something. It could be reading a letter that was written to a friend or the recitation of a poem. Sometimes, it's as simple as creating a picture and using the picture prompt to tell a story or acting out the role of the character in a story. Students also learn how to use transparencies and the overhead projector, how to create posters using technology, and how to use the Microsoft Excel program to make charts and diagrams.

Older students learn how to use reference materials, conduct interviews, create audio and visual presentations, and enhance their presentations through the use of technology. For example, Albert, a sixth-grade student in social studies, worked on a PowerPoint presentation depicting the historical information of the discovery of King Tutankhamun's Tomb after reading *The Secrets of the Tomb* by Linda Lott. He imported pictures from the Internet to enhance his presentation, which he made to an assembly of several fifth-grade classes. Albert prepared his presentation while working on a Kidstation Three activity, and both his written and oral presentation were graded. Each member of Albert's guided reading group gave a presentation on other aspects of this text. Each student knew that he or she was accountable for the work in the kidstation, which would eventually be presented. (See chapter 4 for a discussion of accountability.)

Conclusion

All the activities that are created for the kidstations help the students to develop the essential components of reading, writing, listening, and speaking while teaching students to take pride in their work as they demonstrate or present it to others. The activities at the kidstations were not limited to pencil-and-paper tasks. They incorporated learning experiences that tapped into students' interests and learning and modality preferences. The presentation component motivated the students not only to complete their work but also to work diligently on the quality of the work that they knew could be presented.

The next step is examining the process of implementing a five-day cycle as a means of effectively managing these groups within the classroom. Chapter 4 provides a day-by-day plan within a four-week cycle.

Implementing the Kidstation Model

The emphasis in education today and probably well into the future is accountability. Since the No Child Left Behind initiative began in 2001, greater emphasis has been placed on schools to demonstrate their efforts to be accountable for the education of their students. High-stakes testing and regular benchmark assessments are designed to identify individual student's weaknesses, provide targeted instruction, and support those areas in need of direct instruction (Booher-Jennings, 2006). To ensure that our students become lifelong learners, the students must be part of the accountability equation. Along with administrators, teachers, and parents, students must assume their role in becoming more accountable. Students must be held to high standards of accountability and be called on to demonstrate their competencies as they are learning. While there is certainly a great deal of discussion about this subject, educators are moving toward performance-based and other alternative assessments for students rather than just norm-based testing because they provide authentic assessment and give students the opportunity to demonstrate what they have learned (Capper, Hafner, & Keyes, 2001). The kidstation model provides students with opportunities to use their creative abilities and modality preferences to demonstrate what they have learned.

Student Accountability

As teachers begin to implement the guided reading groups with the appropriate activities in the kidstations, the element of accountability must be clearly established and maintained. Teachers need to change the students' mind-set that these activities are not "busy work" but, rather, extensions of their guided reading session. Their work at these kidstations is evidence or proof that they can apply the skills they are being taught. Furthermore, students are expected to demonstrate their accomplishments on presentation day.

Teachers often ask, How does all of this grouping come together? How do I manage these groups during the literacy block? How do I manage the rest of the class? This looks great on paper, but is this framework really possible? Table 3 provides the five-day model we created for implementing guided reading and the kidstations, but we believe that the best way to explain this model is to share the experience of one of the teachers who implemented it in her classroom. Mrs. Jacobs, an inner-city school teacher, has a very diverse population of 29 students. Recall how we mentioned that students are typically shown many literacy activities during the first few weeks of school. Mrs. Jacobs gives the three remaining groups of students a writing project related to what they had already read in the shared reading group. She has her three groups working independently on creating a diorama depicting the setting of a story the class read together during shared reading. Each student, after making the diorama, has to write a description of the setting in the story using the diorama to help recall and describe the important details of the setting. The students sit at a

Table 3. Five-Day Implementation Model for Guided Reading and the Kidstations

Group	Day 1	Day 2	Day 3	Day 4	Day 5
1	**Guided Reading**	Kidstation One: Word Study	Kidstation Two: Understanding the Literature	Kidstation Three: Responding to the Literature	Presentations
2	Kidstation Three: Responding to the Literature	**Guided Reading**	Kidstation One: Word Study	Kidstation Two: Understanding the Literature	Presentations
3	Kidstation Two: Understanding the Literature	Kidstation Three: Responding to the Literature	**Guided Reading**	Kidstation One: Word Study	Presentations
4	Kidstation One: Word Study	Kidstation Two: Understanding the Literature	Kidstation Three: Responding to the Literature	**Guided Reading**	Presentations

designated area, have the materials they needed, and work independently on their project. They know that they are accountable for completing this project, just as they would be for the work at their kidstations in the days to follow.

Day 1

Group 1— Guided Reading Session

Initially, we recommend that teachers work with one group each day. Mrs. Jacobs begins her first day with the first group while the other three groups work on their diorama project independently. Many grouping models propose that teachers see two guided reading groups each day (Fountas & Pinnell, 2001). However, for very practical reasons, especially having worked with teachers over the years in large-size classes, it's a good idea to start out with one group each day. Again, the teacher must feel comfortable with this process, and it takes time to get the flow of giving brief introductions, setting a purpose, listening to students read, making notations on the chart, interacting with individuals who may need support, and then conducting the follow-up discussion with the group within a 30–35 minute time frame. Realistically, teachers need at least that much time to conduct a meaningful guided reading session. Students also need time to demonstrate how they can read aloud to the teacher and discuss issues related to the purpose of reading. Likewise, the students in the kidstations need a reasonable amount of time to complete the activities that are intended to reinforce or enrich their reading experiences.

In time, as teachers become familiar with the task, the pacing of the session, and the flow of the group, it is possible to meet with more than one group for guided reading. Another point to mention is that the teacher does not necessarily need to listen to every student in the group. A teacher may spend more time with one student than another, but the teacher will make a note of who she did or did not meet with for that session. The next time the group meets, if the same students are in the group, she can listen to the other students. It also is important to note that if a teacher has listened to each student read aloud and the students are not finished reading the text, a teacher can certainly move among the students in the kidstations (other than on the first day) to monitor their progress or address their concerns.

The first group focuses on using keywords from the title and picture clues to make predictions about the story. Students make their predictions before reading the passage and some students adjust those predictions as they read the story. After the students read the story independently, Mrs. Jacobs initiates the discussion with the key questions for their group that address the purpose for reading and then they revisit their predictions. Students share their rationale for making their predictions during the course of the postreading discussion. Mrs. Jacobs asks the students if making predictions helped to improve their comprehension. Several students remark that by using their prior knowledge and context clues to predict how the story would unfold, it helped them to recall and remember details of the story. Mrs. Jacobs also helps students work through some problems they encountered with vocabulary when they read the text.

Group 2—
Guided
Reading
Session

Group 1—
Kidstation
One

Day 2

On the second day, Mrs. Jacobs prepares a word study task for the students in the first group. She bases this activity on the observations she made as the students read with her on the previous day. The students in the first group sit together in a cluster (see Figure 15) and Mrs. Jacobs brings their assignment to them. She places the materials in a box, with enough materials for each student, and stresses the point that all work must be completed by reminding them that she would decide on the project to be presented on the fifth day. In the box of materials are the directions for the activity and a sample of the assignment. The students work on a vocabulary quilt with key words and other related words from the text. Although the students sit in a group, they work independently.

Many times students will ask if they can work together on a group project. We recommend that students work independently in the beginning of the process and most of the time. When students work as a group, there are always some who sit back while others take the initiative for the group. By having students work independently in the beginning of the process, teachers let students know the clear expectations for working at the kidstations, and more important, students learn to be responsible and accountable for their work. On presentation day, if a student has not completed the work at the kidstations and is not ready to give a presentation,

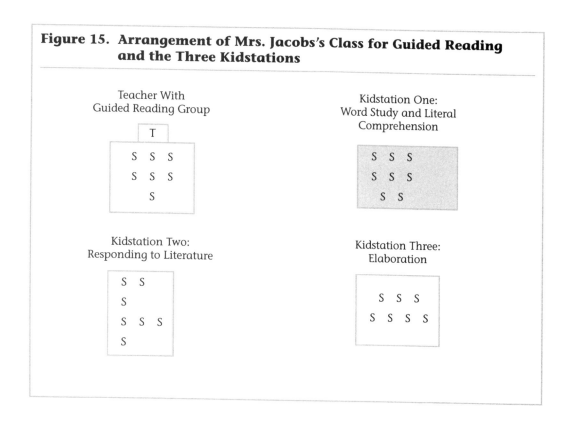

Figure 15. Arrangement of Mrs. Jacobs's Class for Guided Reading and the Three Kidstations

Teacher With
Guided Reading Group

Kidstation One:
Word Study and Literal
Comprehension

Kidstation Two:
Responding to Literature

Kidstation Three:
Elaboration

he or she will be graded accordingly. Typically this won't happen more than once as no student wants to be left out of the presentations. However, a way to prevent this from happening is for the teacher, when he or she is done with the guided reading group discussion, to go to the kidstations and take a minute to assess the students' progress. A literacy specialist, English as a second language (ESL) teacher, special needs teacher, or teacher's aide also can perform the same work to keep students on task. It's not likely that after three days at the kidstations, the student would not have anything to present, but it could happen.

When each student has demonstrated responsibility and accountability and when a project lends itself to it, group work can be initiated. If a teacher does assign a group a cooperative project, we recommend that only one group in the kidstation area work on a cooperative project at a time in order to effectively manage students and maximize student accountability. It also motivates other groups to be accountable when they see another group working cooperatively.

As students in Kidstation One complete their work, they place it in the box and return all the materials and their books, if necessary. Later that day, Mrs. Jacobs collects, checks, and responds to their work. The next day, the students will review her feedback before beginning their task at Kidstation Two.

Meanwhile, Mrs. Jacobs addresses the second guided reading group in the same manner as the first group. The second group uses a different story than the first group and reads the story to determine the main idea using inference skills. The third and fourth groups continue to work on their dioramas.

Group 3—
Guided
Reading
Session

Group 2—
Kidstation
One

Group 1—
Kidstation
Two

Day 3

On the third day, the first group moves to Kidstation Two where their assignment includes determining the elements of the story. Mrs. Jacobs gives the books to the students in the event they want to reread the text, as well as the Story Grammar Wheel Base, the Story Grammar Wheel Overlay, and a paper fastener (see Appendix E, "Story Grammar Wheel Base and Overlay"). After students complete the base, they place the overlay on top of it using the fastener so they see only one element of the story at a time, starting with setting. By focusing on each element separately, students are able to elaborate on each element and then begin to write a first draft of a story summary. Students focus on characters next and continue until they have examined each element.

Next, Mrs. Jacobs assigns the second group their work at Kidstation One. They work on a Seek and Find activity that reinforces their understanding of compound words and contractions (see Appendix E for an example of such an activity, which can be adapted to different stories). After completing the activity, the students use these words in sentences or short paragraphs about the story, using the contractions and compound words they learned.

Then, the third group begins their guided reading session with Mrs. Jacobs. She decides to use the same story as she did with the second group but for a different purpose. Mrs. Jacobs knows that this group needs to develop an understanding of the author's point of view. The students use their ability to analyze the text to provide the evidence to support their interpretation of the author's point of view.

Finally, the fourth group completes their diorama, and they edit and revise their first drafts of their descriptive essays. These students plan to meet with Mrs. Jacobs later in the day before completing their final pieces.

Day 4

Group 4—
Guided
Reading
Session

Group 3—
Kidstation
One

Group 2—
Kidstation
Two

Group 1—
Kidstation
Three

On the fourth day, the first group moves to Kidstation Three where Mrs. Jacbos provides them with a task for elaborating on the skill they were taught in Kidstation Two. At Kidstation Three, students have the opportunity to move beyond the text to apply the skill in different situations. The students select another text and make predictions based on their ability to use the new text clues to validate their predictions. After they read the text, the students provide a rationale for each of their predictions.

Mrs. Jacobs assigns the second group a sequencing activity at Kidstation Two, while the third group, at Kidstation One, is asked to answer the five Ws (who, what, when, where, why) that reinforce literal comprehension. Finally, the fourth group engages in the guided reading session with Mrs. Jacobs. In a short time, Mrs. Jacobs finishes listening to each of the students in the fourth group. She makes several notations regarding a few students in the group and thinks that, although this group may not need an activity at Kidstation One because there were no issues with word recognition, vocabulary, or literal comprehension, she may give them an extended project at Kidstation Two. Subsequently, that is what she decides to do.

Based on their work from Kidstations One and Two and observations of their work in Kidstation Three, Mrs. Jacobs informs each of the students in the first group of which activity she wants them to prepare to present to the class on the following day. Initially, she decides which students would present which activities for several reasons: (1) She wants to capitalize on students' strengths to build their confidence; (2) she wants the class to see a variety of presentations; (3) she wants the presentations to include a variety of media; and (4) by not knowing which assignment Mrs. Jacobs will select, students are inclined to complete all their assignments, further reinforcing their accountability. The first group presents in the first five-day cycle.

Day 5

In the beginning of the process, a different group is scheduled to make their individual presentations each week. Table 4 depicts the rotation of the groups, so that once every four weeks a group is presenting. As their finished product for word study at Kidstation One, the first group in Mrs. Jacobs's class presents their vocabulary quilt (see Appendix E for directions on making a vocabulary quilt). Each student in the group presents the word that he or she was responsible for researching.

The idea of giving an oral presentation can be frightening for some children. The earlier they become comfortable with the process, the better. Some teachers start out by having students view newscasters, talk show hosts, political candidates giving speeches, and even people in commercials, where they see how important it is for them to be good speakers, as well as good readers and writers. This is one way they can come to understand how effective communication skills are an integral part of their literacy development.

It is equally important to model good presentations for students so they are aware of the elements necessary for effective oral communication. This can be done as part of the language arts class where teachers demonstrate voice quality, pronunciation, diction, expression, eye contact, poise, and the appropriate use of

Table 4. The Five-Day Model Incorporated Into a Four-Week Cycle

Week 1					Week 2				
GR	KS-1	KS-2	KS-3	**PR**	GR	KS-1	KS-2	KS-3	
KS-3	GR	KS-1	KS-2		KS-3	**GR**	KS-1	KS-2	**PR**
KS-2	KS-3	GR	KS-1		KS-2	KS-3	GR	KS-1	
KS-1	KS-2	KS-3	GR		KS-1	KS-2	KS-3	GR	

Week 3					Week 4				
GR	KS-1	KS-2	KS-3		GR	KS-1	KS-2	KS-3	
KS-3	GR	KS-1	KS-2		KS-3	GR	KS-1	KS-2	
KS-2	KS-3	**GR**	KS-1	**PR**	KS-2	KS-3	GR	KS-1	
KS-1	KS-2	KS-3	GR		KS-1	KS-2	KS-3	**GR**	**PR**

GR = guided reading group
KS = kidstation
PR = presentation

gestures. When you really stop and think about it, teachers actually engage in these practices every day. However, we don't call the students' attention to these aspects of speaking. Depending on the grade level and type of presentation, teachers also can demonstrate how to create transparencies and use overhead projectors, computers, and simple props in their presentations.

Giving a demonstration is a means for students to develop their oral presentation skills, and it provides teachers with a venue for assessing students' accountability for the work completed at the kidstations. As much as possible, teachers should provide the means and materials for students to incorporate multimedia and technology into their presentations. Oral communication skills, enhanced by the power of technology and multimedia, have become paramount in global society. While for years educators have placed heavy emphasis on reading and writing, we have not approached the development of oral communication with the same vigor (Guastello & Sinatra, 2001). Through the experiences of developing students' presentations, teachers help students develop, refine, reshape, and use oral language as they integrate visual and technological tools. As students engage in conversations and discussions about their work, they learn to be active and attentive listeners as well, in order to respond to other's statements.

Presentations will vary according to length, topic, materials used, and the nature of the activity. It could be a simple prop or puppet animated by a first grader as he recites a fairy tale and talks about the character in the tale or something similar to a show-and-tell by a second grader who creates a flip book to illustrate and retell the sequence of events in a story. After reading several picture books and stories about pumpkins and Halloween, a kindergarten student might make a picture or use a computer software program such as Kid Pix Studio to show how he would grow pumpkins in his backyard. We've watched primary-grade students demonstrate phone etiquette and emergency phone calls after reading books about home safety practices for children. Primary-grade students reading expository leveled readers present weather reports and how-to demonstrations. Third graders have given presentations on how to care for flowers, using props and illustrating the gradual growth of plants using transparencies. The presentations allow for a great deal of integration with content area subject matter. Middle-grade and junior high students may design a costume of a character they wish to portray, or they may draw or import pictures or images from the Internet in their presentations. From using overhead transparencies to creating a PowerPoint presentation with animation, students are given ample time to create and demonstrate the tasks completed at the kidstations. Presentation may include story telling, creating biographical sketches, creating commercials, and designing photo essays on story boards. Students using computer-created semantic maps can explain concepts from both narrative and expository texts. From producing simple diagrams to creating sophisticated graphs, students learn multimedia technology to enhance their presentation skills.

At first, the teachers should orchestrate who presents which completed task. However, as students gain confidence with the process of presenting and demonstrating accountability, they can confer with their teacher in making decisions as to what they would like to present. Pleased with the response of his first-grade students, after three months, Mr. Henry gives a group of students the opportunity to select an activity of their choice for their presentation. Jason uses a transparency he made with the help of the computer to show how he was able to sequence the events in the story using a marker. Marsha makes a book jacket and writes a review of the story she read. Karen displays her vocabulary quilt and explains how she used the thesaurus to complete the activities on the quilt. David creates a PowerPoint presentation depicting a description of the characters in the story. Brian writes several riddles that incorporated the new vocabulary words he learned from this story. Jasmine retells her story summary but in the form of a poem, and Jorge demonstrates how the story grammar wheel helped him write his story summary. Allen acts out his favorite scene in a play he read.

Later, group presentations also can be conducted. For example, a group of third graders explained and demonstrated how to create a fish tank for their classroom after reading about it and visiting the neighborhood pet store. A group of fifth graders presented a panel discussion of the dangers of the greenhouse effect on the environment. Such group discussions at the kidstations allow all students to interact and collaborate on problem-solving skills (Page, 2002), which is the development of the third English language arts standard. Decisions on how and when to make modifications in grouping and presentation types is determined by each student's increased accountability. When students demonstrate their ability to complete their individual activities effectively and responsibly, they are given the freedom to work as a group and select their own projects for presentation.

The presentation aspect benefits not only the students who have developed the task but also the students observing the presentations. Watching and listening to their classmates give the presentations is a means of sharing ideas and is motivational. Figure 16 shows a group of fifth graders presenting to their classmates their autobiographies, while taking great pride in reading portions of the autobiographies and showing how they designed them. Their enthusiasm with this task is contagious, and even the most reluctant writers inquire as to how they might write their own autobiographies.

While their classmates give the demonstration, the rest of the class observes and evaluates the presentation. The process of evaluating is equally important because, in many cases, it supports and affirms the efforts of the students presenting, thus boosting their confidence and self-esteem. In the primary grades, the teacher may use a simple rubric (see Appendix F, "Oral Presentation Evaluation") to evaluate the student's presentation or ask the class (after they finish applauding) to comment on a particular aspect of the presentation, always accentuating the

Figure 16. Students Presenting Their Autobiographies

positive. For example, the following exchange took place in a second-grade classroom:

Mrs. Johnson:	Well, class, what do you think of the way Jason gave his presentation today?
Alice:	Jason, I liked the way you used the puppets to make the story funny.
Jamal:	I could hear Jason, loud and clear.
Jose:	Jason looked at us when he spoke and not at the floor.
Shayna:	Jason, you made the two characters seem so real that I want to read the book now.
Jason:	Thank you (and he took his seat)
Mrs. Johnson:	Well done, Jason, and thank you to those of you who shared your reactions with Jason.

Notice that the teacher initially does not make a judgment on the presentation, which might influence the students' responses. The teacher will meet individually with Jason and review the rubric with him, emphasizing the positive and making a suggestion or two on how to improve on a particular aspect of the presentation. The feedback will enable Jason to improve his future presentations.

With older students, teachers encourage the students to use a rubric (see Appendix F, "Multimedia Presentation Four-Point Rubric") to score their peers and share their observations with those who have presented that day. Subsequently, the teacher individually discusses the presentation with the students, complimenting their strong points and making suggestions for improvement. Sometimes, teachers videotape the students as they give their presentations. Then, the students view the presentation and self-evaluate their performance. This proves to be very effective with older students, who often can determine their needs for improvement along with their teacher and their peers. When teachers provide students with instruction that challenges them to use multimedia and technology in creative ways, they support the enhancement of oral language development and presentation skills (Guastello, 2003).

Audiences for presentations do not need to be limited to the classroom. Presentations can even be part of school assemblies where parents and community leaders are invited to attend. One group of sixth-grade students who read a series of articles on the homeless in major cities in the United States prepared a PowerPoint presentation, complete with statistics about the number of homeless people, and demonstrated how, by using resources within our cities, we could provide homes and work for these individuals. These students invited the mayor and two other officials to the assembly. Presentations such as these give the students a sense of purpose and accomplishment. The opportunities students have to present to varied audiences also helps to reduce the anxiety they feel when they get to high school and college. Speaking and presenting in front of varied audiences, participating in group and individual presentations, and mastering descriptive vocabulary and communicating effectively are essential skills for students from every linguistic and cultural background (Hadaway, Vardell, & Young, 2001). ELLs benefit from the presentations because they provide a forum for students to practice correct syntax and academic language (Guastello & Sinatra, 2001). Presentations not only make the students more accountable for their work but also enhance their oral and written communication skills.

Conclusion

The aspect of student accountability is paramount as teachers initiate the Guided Reading Kidstation Model as a viable learning process. The students' beliefs about their ability to achieve have a direct impact on their learning. They are influenced by the purpose and nature of the tasks, the level of difficulty, the kind of evaluation used to assess their work, and the feedback they receive from their teachers and sometimes their peers (Stipek, 2006). Their self-confidence is improved and maintained by working on tasks that require some effort, challenge, and creativity so that students can complete the tasks at the kidstations and experience a sense of satisfaction and accomplishment. The kidstation model provides students with the opportunity to improve and enrich their learning experiences as they share them with others. The nature of the evaluation focuses on what they have learned and perhaps have mastered and what they need to learn to become more proficient and responsible readers and communicators. Working at the kidstations and eventually presenting their work also gives the students a sense of control in monitoring their progress.

Mrs. Jacobs reported that, in less than two months, all of her students improved in their ability to complete and present their activities from the kidstations. She noted that when she conducted group work in the past, the students might complete 60–70% of the work. After two months, all of her 29 students completed 95–98% of their work. She attributed this increase to the tailored work at the kidstations and the rotation of presentations. Mrs. Jacobs was one of 67 teachers we worked with who noted marked improvement not only in completed work but also in the quality of the finished products their students produced with pride.

Perhaps a contributing factor to the increased productivity of students is the fact that teachers can incorporate other resources in the kidstation model. In chapter 5, we discuss how teachers can utilize the material such as in basal reading series, trade books, leveled books, and textbooks to diversify students' reading experiences and their opportunities for applying their literacy skills. Without reinventing the wheel, we will show how teachers can use readily available materials.

Adapting Basal Readers, Trade Books, Leveled Readers, and Content Area Textbooks to the Kidstation Model

Teachers have the flexibility to use activities from basal readers, trade books, leveled books, and textbooks with the kidstation model. Many of these materials can reinforce skills taught in the guided reading group, such as summarizing, comparing and contrasting, analyzing characters, recognizing figurative language, and determining the author's viewpoint. In addition, many authors of these materials suggest ideas that can be adapted to the kidstation model on their websites, including websites designed by textbook companies, commercial companies, and authors of children's books. Teachers select the activities that best support the needs of a specific guided reading group at the kidstations. When selecting a theme, teachers can match books on the topic to the ability level of each guided reading group, and the activities at the kidstations can provide for reinforcement of skills at the level of the group using the kidstation.

Using Basal Readers With Kidstations

Most basal reading series are organized according to themes. This feature enables the teacher to use the basal reader for the guided reading group, as well as to place some of the activities in the kidstations and adding outside materials on this theme. As an example, Harcourt Horizons develops the theme of American Adventures in its Trophies series (2003) for fifth grade.

Mrs. Jackson, a fifth-grade teacher, uses *What's the Big Idea, Ben Franklin* by Jean Fritz, one of the reading selections from the Trophies series, for her guided reading groups. In addition, she selects, as a read-aloud, *Where Was Patrick Henry on the 29th of May* by Jean Fritz from her classroom library. She discovers that the teacher's manual provides numerous activities for kidstations. She often alternates between the basal reader required by her school district and trade books. She establishes her kidstations so students can see the parallels between Patrick Henry and Benjamin Franklin.

At Kidstation One, knowledge of word recognition, vocabulary, and literal comprehension are reinforced. Mrs. Jackson's students create timelines of the most important events in the lives of both Patrick Henry and Benjamin Franklin.

Kidstation Two involves a summary chart about each patriot taken from the teacher's manual. The sample shown in Figure 17 depicts the chart for Patrick Henry.

After completing their summary charts, students use the information for a second activity, creating word pyramids (see

---

Figure 17. Summary Chart of Accomplishments, Character Traits, and Values for Patrick Henry

What Patrick Henry Accomplished

During his life he was a farmer, a shopkeeper, a lawyer, a politician, and a national hero. He also became a governor of Virginia. On March 23, 1775 he delivered his famous "Give me liberty or give me death" speech at St. John's Church in Richmond, Virginia, which united the colonists to go to war against England. The next year Virginia volunteers marched off to war with Liberty or Death embroidered on their shirtfronts.

Patrick Henry's Abilities and Character Traits

He was a great writer and orator. Patrick Henry believed in fairness. He thought that the King was not fair by the way he lowered the cost of tobacco for the parsons from $.06 to $.02. He fought the case in court and won. He also delivered his famous speech against the King who was once again taxing the colonists unfairly. He said, "Give me liberty or give me death!"

Values Expressed by Patrick Henry

Patrick Henry believed in freedom and fair representation for the people.

From Harcourt Horizons Teacher Edition, New York, Grade 4, Volume 1, ISBN 0153378190. Used with permission from the publisher.

Figure 18) for Patrick Henry and Benjamin Franklin. Students follow a pattern created by Mrs. Jackson: five words about each patriot's childhood, four words about their accomplishments, three words about their character traits, two words about their values, and one word that sums up each man.

To encourage higher order thinking, students are asked to compare and contrast their accomplishments, character traits, and values to those of Patrick Henry and Benjamin Franklin (see Figure 19). The students also indicate which patriot they are most like and why.

Figure 18. Word Pyramid for Benjamin Franklin

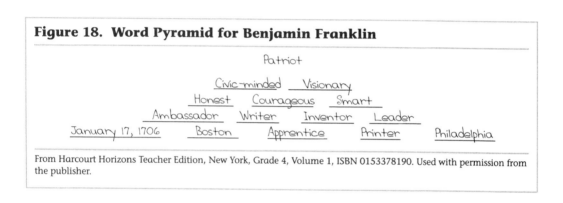

Patriot

Civic-minded   Visionary

Honest   Courageous   Smart

Ambassador   Writer   Inventor   Leader

January 17, 1706   Boston   Apprentice   Printer   Philadelphia

From Harcourt Horizons Teacher Edition, New York, Grade 4, Volume 1, ISBN 0153378190. Used with permission from the publisher.

Figure 19. My Life Comparison Chart

	My Life	Benjamin Franklin	Patrick Henry
Accomplishments	• high grades • good soccer player • raise money to buy books for needy children	• inventor • printer • signer of the Declaration of Independence • ambassador to France • patriot	• farmer • lawyer • orator • governor • patriot
Character Traits	• honest • good friend • like to be helpful • kind	• inquiring mind • believed in justice • wise • intelligent • wanted to improve life for everyone with his inventions and public service	• fought for citizens' rights • believed in liberty • civic-minded—served in public office • role model • radical • patriotic

The activity in Kidstation Three reinforces critical analysis and evaluation. Students are asked to design an award called In Honor of Ben. For this activity, students evaluate the accomplishments or characteristics that should be honored in Franklin's name. Students select the guidelines for eligibility, the prize, and the design of the award. These accomplishments or characteristics include creating an invention or idea to help other people; giving of time, talent, or wealth to help others; and being an honorable and famous American. Mrs. Jackson's students enjoy writing about these items and then designing an award. They decide to vote on some contemporary people to receive this award rather than giving it to other students. These activities emphasize application, analysis, synthesis, and evaluation on Bloom's taxonomy (see chapter 3 for more information on incorporating Bloom's taxonomy with the kidstation activities).

Kidstation Four enables Mrs. Jackson to select from among the activities developed at Kidstations One, Two, and Three for presentation by one of the groups. For example, using the overhead projector one of Mrs. Jackson's groups shows their summary charts of Benjamin Franklin and Patrick Henry.

In addition to the ideas in the teacher's manual, Mrs. Jackson consults the publisher's website for several other suggestions that she adapts to the kidstations. One example found on the website is an interview with Thomas Jefferson. Mrs. Jackson adapts the activity to an interview with Benjamin Franklin and students write as a response to literature for Kidstation Two. After reading *What's the Big Idea, Ben Franklin*, students pretend to be reporters from the fictitious newspaper *The Colonial Times*, and they interview Ben Franklin regarding his accomplishments as an inventor, politician, printer, and writer.

Ideas can also be gleaned from basals for the primary grades. Mr. Marcus, a second-grade teacher, often creates activities for kidstations from the second-grade basal series Macmillan/McGraw-Hill Reading (2003). After selecting a story from Unit 2, "The Bremen Town Musicians," a Brothers Grimm folk tale retold by Margaret H. Lippert, he decides that each guided reading group should read this story in preparation for presenting the story as a puppet play, as suggested in the teacher's manual. However, he emphasizes the skills at each kidstation based on the developmental level of the guided reading group. His objective is to have the students blend and read words with *are, or, ore,* and *ear*. Mr. Marcus focuses on identification of words with these sounds as a teaching point with each guided reading group. For Kidstation One, the advanced readers create their own word sorts with *are, or, ore,* and *ear* on the computer. Students are asked to locate words with these sounds in the story. They also are asked to write a paragraph about the story using words with each sound. At this same kidstation, the average group writes the key words provided in the correct columns of the word sort on the computer, and then they find one word for each column from the story. Next, they select one word from each column and create a sentence using the word. The struggling readers also sort the words in the correct columns on the computer (see Figure 20) and then fill in cloze sentences showing the use of the words as shown in Figure 21. Words for average and struggling reader groups include *care, story, short, dear, scare, morning, near, stare, store,* and *fear.*

For Kidstation Two, each group works on a story web for "The Bremen Town Musicians," as shown in Figure 22. Students note on the story web the elements of the story: where the story takes place (the setting), the main characters, the problem to be solved, and the solution to the problem. By completing the story web, students demonstrate literal comprehension of the story.

Kidstation Three allows students to prepare to act out the story. Mr. Marcus has each group make puppets for their part of the story using the idea presented in the teacher's manual with

---

Figure 20. Word Sort Chart

Fill in the chart below with words that include *are, or, ore,* and *ear.*

are (Example: spare)	or (Example: storm)	ore (Example: snore)	ear (Example: year)
care	short	more	dear
pare	morning	store	fear
mare	story	core	gear
bare	for	tore	hear
dare	nor	fore	near
fare	porch	gore	rear
rare	torch	lore	tear
square		swore	
		score	
		shore	

Figure 21. Cloze Sentences

Write a word from the box to complete each sentence.

| careful scared story for stored morning more hear |

1. Kitty waited _for_ Sally.
2. The loud noises _scared_ us.
3. Mother reads me a _story_ every night.
4. I am _careful_ when I ride my bike.
5. We eat breakfast every _morning_.
6. I'm cold so put on _more_ heat.
7. Luis wanted to _hear_ the song.
8. The clothes are _stored_ in the closet.

Write your own sentence for one of the words in the word box.

Figure 22. Story Web for "The Bremen Town Musicians"

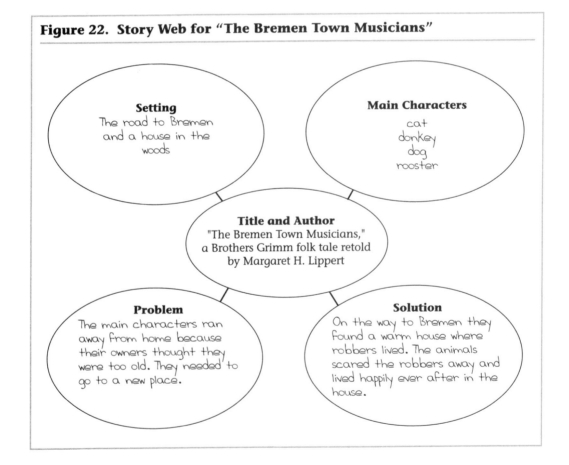

Setting
The road to Bremen and a house in the woods

Main Characters
cat
donkey
dog
rooster

Title and Author
"The Bremen Town Musicians,"
a Brothers Grimm folk tale retold
by Margaret H. Lippert

Problem
The main characters ran away from home because their owners thought they were too old. They needed to go to a new place.

Solution
On the way to Bremen they found a warm house where robbers lived. The animals scared the robbers away and lived happily ever after in the house.

pop sticks and blackline cut-outs of the characters. After making their puppets, the above average readers write the parts for act one collaboratively in their own words. Act two is divided between the average and struggling readers, who practice in their groups after making their puppets.

Kidstation Four provides the opportunity to fulfill language for social interaction. On Friday, Mr. Marcus invites each group to present their portion of the play using the pop stick puppets. This is a variation of the presentation day, which usually highlights one group.

Mr. Marcus also uses the McGraw-Hill website (www.mhschool.com/reading), which includes a companion for this basal and the story "The Bremen Town Musicians." The students are able to access the site when they complete their kidstations. This website features the instruments in an orchestra; other folk tales; and information about farm animals, enjoying jazz, and much more.

Using Trade Books With Kidstations

Trade books lend themselves easily to the kidstation model. Teachers can select books based on a theme with varying readability levels. Here is one instance where a teacher assigns groups by ability when using the same theme. Mrs. Edison involves her sixth-grade class in a study of the Holocaust. Her advanced group reads *Anne Frank: Diary of a Young Girl*, the average group reads *Number the Stars* by Lois Lowry, and the struggling group reads *When Hitler Stole Pink Rabbit* by Judith Kerr. For each book, Mrs. Edison chooses an activity with a similar structure to fulfill each of the standards. For example, each of the guided reading groups completes a character quilt for their story. On the quilt, they list each character in the story with their physical descriptions, feelings, important actions, and traits. Each guided reading group also completes a comparison and contrast chart showing the similarities and differences between two of the main characters in their story.

For Kidstation One, students from each guided reading group create on the computer a character quilt of the main characters in each novel. A character quilt for *Number the Stars* is shown in Figure 23.

Mrs. Olifant, a literacy specialist, joins Mrs. Edison's class two days each week during the literacy block. Her presence enables the struggling readers to receive a guided reading lesson with her once each week and once with Mrs. Edison for a total of at least 80 minutes each week, as opposed to the other groups who receive a minimum of 40 minutes each week. This procedure provides more instruction time for the students who are most in need. Mrs.

Figure 23. Character Quilt for *Number the Stars*

Character	Description	Feelings	Important Actions	Traits
Annemarie	blond tall blue eyes 10 years old	fearful	protected Ellen from the Nazis	brave friendly cautious determined serious
Ellen	dark hair short brown eyes 10 years old	fearful	pretended to be Annemarie's sister Lise	brave serious
Kirsti	curly blond hair 6 years old	happy	told Mrs. Johansen and Mrs. Rosen about being stopped by the soldiers	talkative curious
Mrs. Johansen	good friend and neighbor Christian	anxious fearful	protected Ellen, the Rosens, and other Jews	brave helpful kind
Mrs. Rosen	good friend and neighbor Jewish	anxious fearful	left Ellen with the Rosens and went into hiding	brave
Peter	member of the Resistance Lise's fiancé	anger	worked for the Resistance to try to stop the Nazis	brave trustworthy clever
Uncle Henrik	fisherman who provided a house for the Jews until they left for Sweden	worried	took the Rosens and other Jews to Sweden	brave helpful

Olifant plans the Holocaust unit with Mrs. Edison and supplies several nonfiction books and other materials on the topic for the class. The obvious advantage of this approach is that the students with the greatest needs receive more instruction while remaining in the context of their own classroom.

Mrs. Edison's students then complete a comparison and contrast chart of two of the characters from *Number the Stars*. Figure 24 shows the similarities and differences of two of the main characters, Annemarie and Ellen.

Mrs. Edison selects an activity for Kidstation Three that is a response to literature appropriate for each guided reading group. It involves writing an analytic reaction to story events. The prompts that Mrs. Jackson uses include the following:

- *Anne Frank: Diary of a Young Girl*—If you and your family had to go into hiding, what would you miss most about your present life? Do you and Anne share any of the same feelings?

- *Number the Stars*—Explain how you would protect Ellen from the Nazis if she came to live with your family in Denmark.

- *When Hitler Stole Pink Rabbit*—Compare and contrast Anna and Max's reaction to living in Switzerland after they left Germany.

For Kidstation Three, students write a story about a time when they were afraid. They respond to the following questions: What happened? Who was involved? How was what happened to you the same as or different from the novel that you read?

Figure 24. Comparison and Contrast Chart for *Number the Stars*

Annemarie	Both	Ellen
Christian	Fearful of the Nazis	Jewish
Blond and blue-eyed	Courageous	Dark hair and brown eyes
Tall	10 years old	Short
Has a younger sister named Kirsti	Live in the same apartment building in Denmark	Only child
Athletic	Best friends	Liked to read and study

Mrs. Edison has the opportunity to have students select any of the activities completed at the kidstations for presentation. The Holocaust theme also encourages a social studies integration with research on World War II, geography and maps of the countries involved in the war, and classroom visits by Holocaust survivors. She also provides time for literature circles so that students can have "grand conversations" (Tompkins, 2005) about the books they are reading, the books read by each of the guided reading groups, or both. Literature circles can be held with the whole class or in small groups. By using this forum, students have the opportunity to share their personal responses about the selection.

Using Leveled Texts With Kidstations

Leveled texts are collections of books that are used by students during independent and guided reading. They are organized and categorized according to characteristics that make them easier or harder to read. Text levels are created on a continuum that supports a child's use of strategies and offers problem-solving opportunities that build the reading process (Fountas & Pinnell, 1996). Teachers can develop activities to be used in conjunction with the kidstation model as a follow-up to the use of leveled texts. These activities can specifically address the vocabulary and skills targeted in the leveled text. For example, Scott Foresman provides leveled readers from level 1 to level 180, encompassing grades 1 through 6. Each text focuses on two or three words and a comprehension skill. For example, *The New Kid* by Kari James, a leveled reader 74A, is appropriate for third grade. It highlights the vocabulary *brave*, *afraid*, *spelling*, and *reservation*, and targets the comprehension skill of visualizing for development in this realistic fiction story.

After working with the students in the guided reading group and taking a running record, Mr. Gomez, a third-grade teacher, decides that the students should do a vocabulary graph and a four-square vocabulary at Kidstation One because these activities, which students are familiar with, help meet the first English language arts standard. For the vocabulary graph, Mr. Gomez creates a graphic organizer on the computer for the word *brave*. Students use their hard-copy thesaurus and an online version to locate synonyms and antonyms for *brave*, as well as to determine the part of speech for the word. Students also supply examples to show their understanding of *brave*, such as "rescuing a drowning person" or "firefighter fighting a fire." They also place other forms of the word like *bravely*, *braver*, and *bravest* on the organizer. Finally, they create an illustration to show the meaning of *brave* (see Figure 25).

For the four-square vocabulary experience, the students divide a sheet of paper into four parts. On each fourth of the paper, they accomplish a different task involving the word *afraid* from *The New Kid* to show their understanding of the word. They write what they think the word means, use the dictionary to write the word in syllables and list the part of speech, write their own sentence for the word, and illustrate the meaning of the word (see Figure 26).

The activity for Kidstation Two involves developing a story map with picture panels for *The New Kid* (see Figure 27). The story map helps the students to sequence the events of the story. Mr. Gomez selects this activity to reinforce the skill of visualizing. The students visualize what happens to the new girl in the school and

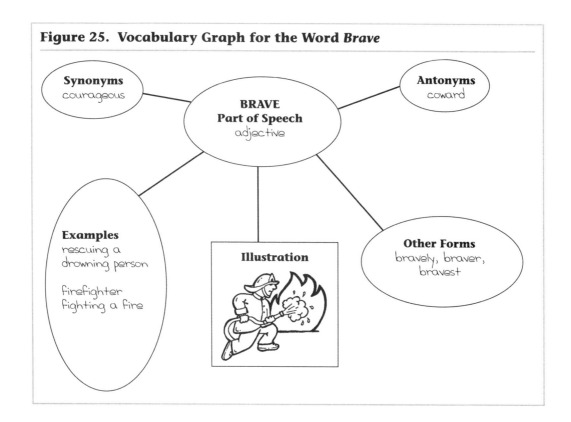

Figure 25. Vocabulary Graph for the Word *Brave*

Synonyms
courageous

BRAVE
Part of Speech
adjective

Antonyms
coward

Examples
rescuing a drowning person

firefighter fighting a fire

Illustration

Other Forms
bravely, braver, bravest

Figure 26. Four-Square Vocabulary Experience

Square 1

afraid p. 16

Read the word in context.
Based on how this word is used in the story and the picture clues, this is what I think the word means:

I think the word means to be frightened.

Square 2
Now look in the dictionary. Write the word in syllables and the part of speech.

a•fraid–adjective

List the meanings for the word.

frightened, scared, fearful, terrified, anxious, troubled

Square 3
Now write your own sentence with the new word. Write it with enough clues in the sentence so that someone who doesn't know the word can tell what the word means by your context clues.

When my bedroom is very dark, I am afraid.

Square 4
Illustrate the new word. Draw, cut out, or download a picture.

then find graphics on the computer or draw their own pictures that help show the sequence of the events in the story. Some students prefer to draw the pictures and then describe each one with a written statement while other students prefer to begin by writing the events and then drawing them.

Mr. Gomez begins Kidstation Three, which is based on critical analysis and evaluation, by having the students write a letter on the computer to the main character in the story from her old school giving her advice about how to make new friends (see Figure 28). Three ideas have to be included in the letter. Because the main character in the story is not given a name, the students are asked to name her in their letter.

For the presentation at Kidstation Four, some students share their vocabulary activities and others present their story maps or read their letters. Mr. Gomez emphasizes speaking loudly, slowly, and clearly. His students are always an appreciative audience, making one another feel valued when they present their material.

Kidstations also can be effective when using leveled text in the upper elementary grades. For example, Mr. Chu, a sixth-grade

Figure 27. Story Map for *The New Kid*

Picture Panels   Writing Panels

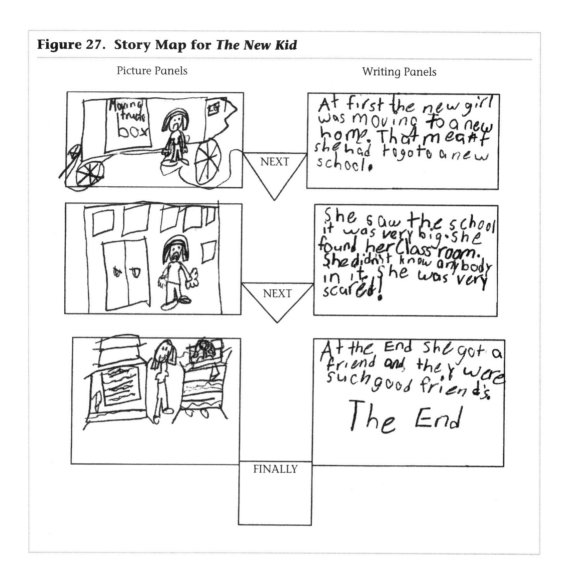

At first the new girl was moving to a new home. That meant she had to go to a new school.

NEXT

She saw the school it was very big. She found her classroom. She didn't know anybody in it. She was very scared!

NEXT

At the End she got a friend and, they were such good friends.

The End

FINALLY

teacher, prepares kidstation activities for *The Mystery of the Gold Pen* (level 178A), another Scott Foresman leveled text on the sixth-grade level. The story features the vocabulary words *arc*, *calculate*, *formula*, *scholar*, and *sphere*. The comprehension skill listed for this text is using graphic sources because students are asked to collect and organize data on a chart to solve the mystery.

For Kidstation One, Mr. Chu asks the students to categorize the new vocabulary according to each word's part of speech. Next, he asks students to prepare a crossword puzzle using each new word.

At Kidstation Two, the students put the events of the story in the proper sequence and then create a PowerPoint presentation to

Figure 28. Letter to Best Friend

Directions: Pretend you are the best friend of the girl who moved to the new school. Write her a friendly letter giving her at least three ideas about how to make friends in her new school.

Date

Dear Maria,

    I moved to a new school last year. It was very hard to meet new friends. I made many new friends by using some ideas that my mom shared with me.

    These are a few ideas that might help you. First, I joined a baseball team. That really helped since the kids invited me to their houses to practice. The next thing I did was set up a lemonade stand in front of my house. A lot of kids stopped by to talk and to work with me. I donated the money that I made to buy books for homeless people. The third thing I did was bring my pet snake to school with the teacher's permission. The other kids were really interested and asked me a lot of questions.

    I hope that I have helped you. Please write to me to let me know how you are doing in your new school.

Your friend,

Juan Lopez

retell the story. Each group member is responsible for creating specific scenes on the PowerPoint.

In Kidstation Three, Mr. Chu capitalizes on students' natural interest in mysteries. He provides them with a plot word list from which they are to choose one element from each category to write their own original mystery story (see Figure 29). As a second activity at Kidstation Three, the skill of using graphic sources is reinforced. Using the website Mystery Net's Kids Mysteries (http://kids.mysterynet.com), the students select a mystery to solve. They follow the same procedure as the students in the leveled text *The Mystery of the Gold Pen* by creating a chart to gather the data to solve the mystery (see Figure 30).

The students share their original mysteries, PowerPoint presentations, and their solutions to the website mysteries on the presentation days for Kidstation Four.

Many resources can be found in the teacher's manuals for basals, trade books, and leveled books; however, teachers also

Figure 29. Create a Mystery

Please select one or more words from each column to write your own mystery.

Setting	Character	Motive	Weapon
School	Doctor	Revenge	Machine gun
Castle	Rock star	Insane	Bomb
Garden	Soldier	Accident	Poison
Beach	Spy	Money	Suffocation
Jungle	Judge	Love	Rope
Desert	Detective	Jealousy	Pipe or club
Mountains	Forensics expert	Temper	Knife
City	Football player	Terrorism	Car
Your choice	Your choice	Your choice	Your choice

Figure 30. Graphic Organizer for Mystery Data for "The Case of the Disappearing Dimes"

Things We Know	Things We Need to Find Out
Harvey, Waldo's assistant, made a low salary.	Who took the rare coins? Which person had the opportunity to open the safe and get the coins?
Fiona, Waldo's sister, was inheriting the house and everything in it.	Where are the coins hidden?
Mr. Baxter, the lawyer, would not have told Dad about the rare coins if he intended to steal them.	Who would benefit most from stealing the rare coins?

should develop their own original materials for the kidstations. By collaborating with other teachers on their grade level and the school specialists, a wealth of materials can be developed. Table 5 lists additional ideas that can be employed at each kidstation for the primary and intermediate grades.

Using Content Area Textbooks With Kidstations

The diversity in today's elementary school classrooms provides a challenge for teachers when using content area textbooks because they typically have a higher readability level than the designated grade level. It is not uncommon for teachers to find supplementary

Table 5. Additional Ideas for Kidstations Based on Grade Level

Grade Level	Word Recognition (Kidstation One)	Vocabulary Development (Kidstation One and Two)	Literal Comprehension (Kidstation One)	Response to Literature (Kidstation Two)	Critical Analysis and Evaluation (Kidstation Three)
Grades 1–3	• Create word posters • Organize word clusters • Complete word sorts • Create word chains • Add affixes (prefixes and suffixes) • Write and illustrating homophones, homographs, and heteronyms • Add to word walls • Learn and apply spelling patterns • Add to "Words I Want to Learn to Spell"	• Categorize word sorts • Explain literal meanings • Analyze figurative language • Complete concept maps • Write possible sentences • Complete analogies • Create hink pinks (e.g., unhappy father—sad dad, uncovered seat— bare chair)	• Construct a story map • Respond to the story • Map characters • Create a movie (based on a book) using a paper roll • Create pictures or a comic strip to retell the story • Create a mobile to illustrate the book • Make a mural of the book	• Complete story boards • Create open-mind portraits, which show the face of a character on one page and the mind of the character on the second page with words the character might have said and pictures of events from the story • Write retellings of stories • Create setting maps • Respond in a journal	• Write a review of a book • Write the story from another point of view • Explain what you learned from the book • Write a new ending • Explain how the story made you feel
Grades 4–6	• Analyze word structure • Create word sorts • Find word origins • Put together word collections • Generate words • Understand idioms	• Compare characters and stories by listing them, grouping them, and then labeling them • Create semantic word maps or webs	• React to QAR— Question-Answer Relationships, a strategy developed by Raphael (1986) that encourages students in the text and in their background knowledge when answering questions	• Write dialogue for characters • Respond in a journal • Write Readers Theatre scripts	• Write higher level questions based on Bloom's taxonomy (i.e., analysis, synthesis, and evaluation)

(continued)

Table 5. Additional Ideas for Kidstations Based on Grade Level (continued)

Grade Level	Word Recognition (Kidstation One)	Vocabulary Development (Kidstation One and Two)	Literal Comprehension (Kidstation One)	Response to Literature (Kidstation Two)	Critical Analysis and Evaluation (Kidstation Three)
Grades 4–6	• Explain metaphors and similes • Find and explain borrowed words from other cultures • Explain the author's style or trademark • Write acronyms • Use blended words	• Categorize vocabulary in word sorts • Write questions using Bloom's taxonomy • Complete semantic feature analysis maps (i.e., charts used to classify words according to distinguishing characteristics) • Create concept cards for new vocabulary terms and compete in teams or concept circles to supply definitions, examples, and so forth • Create word analogies • Complete cloze passages • Complete context puzzles • Find word definition puzzles	• Understand sentence-level comprehension • Answer anticipation guides used to preview the story • Use structured overviews • Create K-W-L charts • Participate in reciprocal teaching, a strategy developed by Palincsar and Brown (1984) that promotes comprehension through predicting, generating questions, summarizing, and clarifying	• Create cause and effect chains, a flow chart showing how one cause can have multiple effects or lead to other cause and effect situations • Apply story to one's own life • Interpret political cartoons or create cartoons that show historical events or events related to contemporary issues • Write sequels • Compare two stories • Create headlines and write newspaper articles about stories	• Analyze characterization, author's purpose, appropriateness for audience, timeliness, accuracy, and so forth

materials appropriate for their students to use in conjunction with such texts. Further, guided reading groups in the kidstation model can be arranged by reading level to ensure that all children understand the content area material. In addition to struggling readers, the inclusive classroom may contain students with learning disabilities as well as ELLs. These learners often have difficulty reading social studies and science textbooks. The kidstation model can be adapted to meet these learners' needs. The teacher can provide instruction reading the textbook using a guided reading format, and the kidstations can be structured to reinforce reading and social studies skills based on the needs of the students in the class.

Ivey (1999) reported that readers who struggled with grade-level and whole-class content area work enjoyed reading when the text was at their level and when they worked in smaller groups using a guided reading approach. This approach allows students to engage in text at an appropriate challenge level but one that does not exceed their skill level. For ELLs, small-group instruction that involves talk about content being studied in social studies and science helps them get a sense of what is acceptable culturally and socially in their new linguistic environment. In the small-group setting, the teacher can more effectively observe, monitor, and attend to the needs of individual readers (Strickland, Ganske, & Monroe, 2002).

To illustrate how easily the model can be adapted for use with specialists, let us return to Mr. Marcus and his second graders. Mr. Marcus is an inclusion teacher whose classroom contains five students with learning disabilities. Mrs. King, the special education teacher, works with him in the morning during his 90-minute literacy block, instructing guided reading or kidstations for these five students. Initially, Mrs. King collaborated with Mr. Marcus on the story and skill that the five inclusion students would be working on during their guided reading group and the reinforcement activities in the kidstation. With this kind of collaboration, it is possible for Mrs. King to frequently conduct the guided reading group or, at other times, monitor the students at the kidstations.

After lunch, Mr. Marcus teaches science and social studies with only his aide's assistance. To address the needs of these students, Mr. Marcus conducts a guided reading lesson using the Macmillan/McGraw-Hill textbook for second grade, *We Live Together* (2003). In other words, he preteaches the portion of the text that he will be using with the whole class after working with this group. Mr. Marcus is pleased with this approach because he discovered that his learning disabled students become more actively involved in the whole class lesson after the guided reading group. They are able to read the material, understand the new vocabulary, and comprehend the concepts presented. While working with these students, the remainder of the class is actively involved in kidstations that reinforce reading and previously learned social studies skills. His aide monitors each group's progress. One of the special education students, Jennifer, remarks that she feels "smarter" this year. She comments that she is able to raise her hand "a lot" during the lesson because she knows the meanings of the words and what the social studies story is about.

Mr. Marcus uses the guided reading group with the special education students to preteach Lesson One, "America's First People" from *We Live Together*, and then he introduces the same text to the remainder of the class. After all of the students have read and discussed the text, Mr. Marcus creates kidstations from the teacher's manual, and he and his aide monitor the students while they work at the kidstations.

In Kidstation One, the students focus on the skill of using charts to gain information. Students examine a chart showing Native American groups to discern their clothing and types of homes. They record the information on their own charts, shown in Figure 31. For Kidstation Two, the students draw and explain a favorite family custom or celebration, an activity based on an idea

---

Figure 31. Native American Matrix

Name of Group	Type of Clothing	Description of Their Homes
Yurok	Plain animal skins	Wood house
Lakota Sioux	Buffalo animal skins with fringes and feathered headdress	Tepee
Iroquois	Fringed animal skin and feathered headdress	Long house
Navajo	Cloth cape and blanket	Round house
Caddo	Animal skins and feathered cape	Dome-shaped house
Cherokee	Colorful animal skins with fringes	Round house with straw roof

From Macmillan/McGraw-Hill Social Studies: *We Live Together*. © 2003. Used with permission from the publisher.

in the teacher's manual. At Kidstation Three, students use the story "America's First People" to identify the traditions of the Yurok Native Americans. Then using a comparison chart (see Figure 32), students analyze Yurok traditions and their own traditions to determine which are alike and which are different.

Ms. Pakula also uses the kidstation model when she teaches her fourth-grade students social studies. She has a cluster of six ELLs in her class. Like Mr. Marcus, she preteaches them the content of the social studies lesson before working with the whole class. Since Ms. Pakula has all of the fourth-grade ELLs in her class, the English as a Second Language (ESL) teacher, Mr. Mojeda, joins her for social studies and/or science instruction. He either works with the six students at their kidstations or conducts a preteaching session on the text material that will be introduced to the class. Since the fourth graders will be taking an English language arts state test in the next few months, Ms. Pakula and Mr. Mojeda design kidstations to reinforce several reading skills and fulfill the English language arts standards while addressing social studies content.

Ms. Pakula and Mr. Mojeda both use activities from the *Harcourt Horizons* (2003) fourth-grade social studies textbook to strengthen reading skills. Kidstation One reinforces for students the idea of locating information and literal comprehension skills by using a current-events graphic organizer with articles written on each group's reading level. This graphic organizer, which is taken from the teacher's manual, involves the summary of an important event (who, what, when, where, how, and why), as well as a prediction, comparison, and personal reaction. Mr. Mojeda selects articles from children's magazines written at levels lower than fourth grade to ensure his students' success, and students use these articles to complete the graphic organizer. Mr. Mojeda supports

Figure 32. Traditions

Yurok Traditions	Shared Traditions	My Traditions
canoeing	canoeing	canoeing
fishing	fishing	fishing
making baskets	singing	going on vacation
telling stories	dancing	
singing songs		
dancing		

From Macmillan/McGraw-Hill Social Studies: *We Live Together.* © 2003. Used with permission from the publisher.

students by offering them assistance (as needed) in locating key words that help them to identify the who, what, when, where, why, and how in the articles. Another activity at Kidstation One reinforces students' vocabulary of land and water forms. Mr. Mojeda copies vocabulary cards from the teacher's manual with the vocabulary word on one side and the meaning on the other side. The ELLs test each other on the words. Mr. Mojeda uses a Bingo game to quiz the students. Finally, the students create a mural with the land and water forms, which they label.

At Kidstation Two, the skill of summarizing is highlighted. Mr. Mojeda shows the ELLs how to find the main points in the story *Landscape Formed by Glaciers*. They work on this activity together to write a coherent summary, which Mr. Mojeda writes on chart paper.

When students work at Kidstation Three, they participate in an activity that further advances their ability to evaluate and improve their writing skills. As suggested in the teacher's manual, each student chooses a physical feature of New York, such as a river, mountain, lake, or forest, and they write an advertisement to persuade people to visit it. They also use illustrations. Figure 33 shows a group of students working on their advertisements.

Figure 33. Students Creating Advertisements

For Kidstation Four, the students share their advertisements. Both Ms. Pakula and Mr. Mojeda agree that the ELLs exhibit pride and enthusiasm with lots of expressive language as they shared their advertisements.

Pablo comments on how much he likes having Mr. Mojeda come to his classroom:

> Mr. Mojeda is a cool guy. He is helping me to learn English and read the social studies book. It is fun to work at the kidstations. You do lots of neat stuff. I liked working on the advertisement. When I grow up, I want to be a news reporter.

Ms. Pakula and Mr. Mojeda work extremely well as a team to support the progress of their ELLs. However, Ms. Pakula also uses the kidstations with all of her students without Mr. Mojeda's presence. She states that the small-group structure provided by the kidstation model enables her to address the individual needs of her students rather than working in a whole-class structure with the social studies textbook.

Conclusion

The kidstation model supports the teacher's need to follow the standards and to ensure ongoing authentic assessment of his or her students. Activities can be crafted from many sources that focus on the specific needs of all types of learners from the struggling reader to the gifted reader. Teacher's manuals, websites, and book guides, as well as teacher-made materials, can be adapted to the kidstation model for literacy and content area instruction.

As we know, teaching and learning are reflective processes. When teachers initially start to implement the kidstation model in their classrooms, they often pose questions. Unless teachers have the benefit of actually witnessing the demonstrations prior to implementing the kidstation model, they typically have many questions. And, of course, unique situations arise. Chapter 6 deals with such questions and provides our answers.

The Kidstation Model: Q & A

Quite often when teachers read about this topic of guided reading and student accountability, they try to imagine this model being implemented in their classrooms. The model presented in this text is designed to assist the teachers with the logistics of implementing guided reading. The size of the groups, the number of groups, and the length of time with each group lends itself to a thorough and effective development of guided reading practices in the classroom. Simple checklists make it possible for teachers to monitor the children's progress and address their specific needs. If teachers experience difficulty managing the guided reading groups, the process tends to collapse. This book is intended to address the practical aspects of conducting guided reading groups in response to the challenges teachers have encountered. The element of student accountability enables teachers to evaluate authentic work produced by their students.

Since our article "Student Accountability: Guided Reading Kidstations" (Guastello & Lenz, 2005) was published, we have received many requests for staff development, inquiries about the model, and positive feedback from teachers in school districts across the United States. This chapter provides a sampling of actual questions and comments from teachers in response to our staff development on guided reading kidstations and from our article. We hope that some of these questions and answers are helpful to you as you think about implementing the model.

Q: I am a first-grade teacher in an urban school. I have 26 students in my class. Although I am very interested in your model, I am not sure that it will work with first graders, especially with the size of my class.

A: We suggest that you begin the kidstation model in November when the students are acclimated to first grade and your routines. Activities in the kidstations can be created and drawn from shared readings and read-alouds. At this stage, students should have modeled and worked through a few story grammar wheels and story boards, as well as word sorts, search-and-find word recognition activities, retellings through pictures, and character mapping. These activities work well in the kidstations in the early portion of the year. As the students become more proficient readers, they are capable of doing most of the activities that we have included in the book independently as they apply the activities to other stories.

Q: As a teacher of first graders, I know that many of my students would not be ready for the kind of activities you described for Kidstations Two and Three. They can just about write sentences. Does that mean they can only go to one kidstation?

A: No, not at all. You can put any activities you want into those kidstations. Much of first grade is developing word recognition skills, vocabulary, and literal comprehension. Each of these areas can be addressed in each of the three stations.

Q: I teach fifth grade in a diverse school district. Fifty percent of my students are English-language learners. I love the idea of the kidstations, but I am wondering if my ELLs can work for sustained periods productively.

A: In our staff development program in both the South Bronx and Manhattan, we had a preponderance of ELLs. The maximum amount of time that students generally work at a kidstation is 30–35 minutes. These activities have been previously modeled for the students, and they have had opportunities to work with their ESL teacher prior to engaging in the activity in the kidstation where they are expected to function independently. In some school districts, the ESL teachers often are able to work in the classroom during the literacy block to assist these students. The ESL teachers also provided activities appropriate for these students that could be used to supplement the teachers' materials.

Q: The kidstation model is a neat idea; however, I am a new teacher who already feels overwhelmed by the amount of daily preparation and accountability for the number of state and local assessments.

A: We understand your situation completely. You know that time on task with meaningful literacy activities will actually improve your students' scores. Collaboration with the other teachers at your grade level can reduce your workload for the preparation of the materials. If you are using a basal program, you can adapt the activities to the kidstations. (We provide some examples from actual basal series in chapter 5.) Each week you can work on activities for a story and then share these activities with your colleagues. In no time you will have ample activities for the kidstations.

Q: I like your five-day cycle with the presentations for student accountability. I am a sixth-grade teacher who believes that students don't get enough opportunities to present their work. My concern is that when students see what other children have done with the activity at the kidstation, they may have a tendency to copy the idea when they present. Another problem is that those students who present later have an unfair advantage since they have seen samples.

A: You want your students to see good models of work. It is beneficial for your struggling readers to see some examples of high quality products; therefore, let your stronger students present first. They will not be completing the activity on the same piece of literature, so you can evaluate the work they have done. The purpose is to improve their ability to demonstrate what they have created at their kidstation, and because the activities are deigned to address the needs of the students, the mode of presentation may be similar but the content is different. This is not a competitive situation. In the beginning, the teacher determines what and how the material is presented to avoid redundancy of the mode of presentation. Some students may need to imitate in the beginning, but eventually, as their confidence as presenters increases, they will want to shine in their own light.

Q: How often do you change the activities in the kidstations? Is it per story or longer when introducing a new skill?

A: The kidstation activities change according to the story you are using and the skill you wish to have the students develop. If you determine that the students need further reinforcement of that same skill, you can use another story with a similar activity.

Q: I am thinking about implementing your kidstation model; however, I have a very chatty third-grade class that has difficulty working independently. I don't want to be interrupted while working with the guided reading group.

A: Begin by modeling the kinds of activities they will complete in the kidstations and providing students with opportunities to do these with you so that they will be able to accomplish these tasks by themselves (see chapter 4). For the first half of the school year, insist on silent independent work at the kidstations. When the students become responsible for maintaining their focus, then you can permit more collaboration. You also can assign a leader at each group who is responsible for explaining the activity to members of the group. After working with your guided reading group, you will want to check the status of each group's accomplishments. Points can be awarded to the groups that worked most responsibly. These points can be traded for computer time and special presentations. For example, one group of students wanted to present a rap song they created after reading a story about baseball legend Jackie Robinson. Because they earned points for working responsibly, they were able to make their special presentation.

Q: I am a sixth-grade teacher, and I know that many students at that age (11–12) are self-conscious about presenting in front of their peers. The four-day model works great, but when it comes to the fifth day for the presentations, that's where I am meeting resistance from a few of my students who are terrified to present. They do the work and it is done well, but they are just afraid to present in front of their peers. Any suggestions?

A: This is precisely why children need to be given the opportunity to use their oral language presentation skills as early as kindergarten! It's not uncommon for students who have not been accustomed to giving presentations to feel anxious about doing so. Start by allowing the student to present to a classmate friend. Observe as the student explains his or her work and then grade the student for the presentation. As part of the evaluation, recommend that the next time he or she presents, the student must select three additional students to present to in a small group. Each time the student presents, increase the size of the group until the student is, in fact, presenting to the entire group. In the meantime, assist the student as much as possible with positive feedback. Gradually, the student's confidence will increase and their anxiety will decrease. We have found this strategy to be most effective with ELLs who are sometimes self-conscious about their language ability. As their English becomes more proficient, they gain a comfort level with presenting in front of their peers.

Q: I teach third grade. I think this model is very practical and sound. It has enabled me to work much more effectively with my guided reading groups. Not only do I see more of their work being completed but also my students really seem to be taking pride in their work. The presentation aspect is a major motivating factor. My question is this: If I am working with my group three and the focus of the reading is to develop and discuss the skill of drawing conclusions, and I determine that two of the students have not grasped the concept, do I still send them to the kidstations?

A: Good question! Here's where flexible grouping comes in. When you are finished with this group and it is time for them to go to their kidstations, there are several options. One, if the student needs work with word recognition or vocabulary and you have activities for that at Kidstation One, then send the student to the kidstation.

The next day, when you are working with the fourth group, if they are working on the same skill but a different story, include the two students from the third group into the fourth group where they will have the opportunity to read a new story and see how the concept is developed in the new story. Perhaps by listening to and joining in on the discussion about drawing conclusions with the fourth group, these students can now go on to their own group for Kidstations Two and Three.

Two, teach the skill again in a shared reading group before letting these students go on to Kidstations Two and Three.

Q: If I am grouping my students by ability, how do the groups change?

A: As we discuss in chapter 2, you also can group by skill and by interest. In fact, in order to motivate students and give them the chance to appreciate others' interests, once in awhile, group by interests. Let's say you have six students who are science fiction buffs. You can have them bring in something they like to read. Your focus for the group may be differentiating between fact and fiction. Your kidstation activities would be geared toward word recognition as it pertains to their book. For instance, they may create a crossword, select 10 words and make picture concept cards, or create their own Seek and Find and challenge their group members with it. For Kidstation Two, they can write a character description or describe the role of a character. For Kidstation Three, they can identify elements of the story that are fact and those that are fiction. Then, given our rapid growth of technology, explain what fictional aspect of the book could become real. Each of the students in this group may be reading at different levels, and that's great. They would now be working and discussing the topic with students with whom they may not ordinarily be working with if you kept grouping by ability only, which we do not encourage.

Q: To my amazement, my fourth graders have really taken to this model. They keep asking me when they can work on a group project. When do I let that happen, and how often?

A: We're glad to hear that the students are enjoying this model and that it's working well. The students have to demonstrate their individual ability to be responsible for their own work. Usually, by January, some students may be ready to work as a group. Here are some guidelines.

For older students, first have the group submit a proposal to you. They must state the purpose of the group, name the book they wish to read, what materials they will need, the activities for the kidstation, and most important, the responsibilities of each member of the group. They should know that they will be graded individually based on the description of their contribution and as a group. We would encourage one group project a month, each month from a different group. For younger students, you should set the guidelines for group work. If students are able to work responsibly, we encourage the use of group work because it is beneficial to students.

Q: I understand that when the students complete their work, they are to put it in a box. Do I have to correct everything they do?

A: Human nature being what it is, students will not think their work is important if you are not going to respond to it. You also are sending a message that it is not important if you don't respond to it. So, yes, to answer your question, you should be responding to their work. Notice, we use the word *responding* because not everything needs to be graded. There's a difference. Remember, three different groups are working at three different kidstations. Let's say you have six students in each group. Students in Kidstation One are working on homophones with picture clues. Another group is writing their response to a shared inquiry questions in Kidstation Two, and the third group is working on their PowerPoint presentation. At the end of the day, I may grade the second group's work, but for the first and third groups, I may look over their work and write a quick and encouraging response. But the next day, everyone gets their work back that has been *responded* to by the teacher.

Q: I have 30 students in an inclusion class in an inner-city school. I am expected to conduct guided reading groups. I would love to see this work, but I don't know where to start.

A: We imagine that you must have other teachers in the room with you. The first thing you need to do is sit with them to do some collaborative planning so that activities for this diverse group can be realistically created to meet their academic needs and time factors. Sometimes the special teachers will modify an activity for the specials education students. They are still developing the intended skill, but these teachers can provide the appropriate help for the student at the kidstations.

Q: I really like the idea that the students have to present their work. It allows the students with various learning preferences to be creative. But how and when do I teach them about presentations and how to use the computer or audiovisual equipment?

A: Teaching the students how to give a presentation is part of their language arts lessons where they learn to use oral presentation skills. In some schools, teachers invite guest speakers to model a presentation or they model it themselves. Teaching the students how to work on transparencies with overhead projectors also can be part of their technology training, which is another example of collaborating with the technology staff in your school.

Q: I am a third-grade teacher who wants to try your model. Unfortunately, in my school district, we are required to work with each guided reading group every day. I have four groups, so you can imagine how overwhelmed I feel by the end of the day. I don't feel I have enough time to address the needs of my students. I believe that your model would enable me to give more quality time to each group rather than rushing through four groups. Do you have any ideas as to how I can convince the administrators and supervisors to allow me to try your model?

A: We suggest that you give them a copy of our article (Guastello & Lenz, 2005) or a copy of this book so that they can see the advantages of using the kidstation model. You might enlist the cooperation of your colleagues on the third-grade level. You can suggest a pilot of the model that the administrators could observe to see firsthand its effectiveness.

Q: How have students responded to the kidstation model?

A: Reggie, a second-grade student, said that he really enjoys the kidstations because he can work on his own: "I like the chance to draw and then write my stories, and I love making my own books."

Vanessa, a third-grade student, commented that she enjoys having time to talk to her teacher during the guided reading sessions, with no one interrupting them. "All my friends are busy at the kidstations. It gives me a chance to talk to my teacher about what I am reading."

Two of Mrs. Edison's sixth-grade students, Shanika and Joshua, commented about their participation in the kidstation model during their student of the Holocaust. Shanika remarked, "Working independently at the kidstations made me feel more grown up." She stated that she believed that she learned more because she had a chance to do an activity about what she was reading. She further stated that she was always very "shy" about presenting in front of the class, but this year she was proud to present the work that she created in the kidstation. This was evidenced in a powerful story that she wrote about having to hide when she thought that someone was breaking into her apartment. She empathized with how Anne Frank must have felt hiding day after day.

Joshua mentioned that he didn't know anything about the Holocaust before this study. He said that the guided reading groups, kidstation activities, and using the Internet gave him a better understanding of the horror of the Holocaust, World War II, and what it was like to live during that time. He said, "The books that we read made the Holocaust clearer to me rather than reading about it in our social studies textbook."

Final Thoughts

Our purpose in writing this book is to provide a model for teachers that gives them and their students the time to work together on literacy activities while encouraging teacher reflection and active involvement on the part of students. Through using the kidstation model, teachers are able to learn more about each student from the sustained periods of guided reading and thus able to create reinforcement in needed skill areas that encourage reading, writing, listening, speaking, and viewing. In addition, teachers can set appropriate, high expectations for student accountability while addressing state and national standards for literacy instruction.

As former teachers and administrators at the elementary level and now professors of literacy courses at the college level, we are keenly aware of the planning and implementation needed for a successful literacy program in any classroom. We hope that the ideas we share here will make the task less demanding and more enjoyable for you and your students. Please continue to share your thoughts with us about the model. Our goal is to continue to refine it to meet your needs.

Literacy Profiles

Literacy Profile for Primary Grades

Name _____ Grade _____ Year _____

Qualitative Reading Inventory:

Word Recognition
____Independent   ____Instructional   ____Frustration Level

Narrative Text Comprehension
____Independent   ____Instructional   ____Frustration Level
____Listening Potential

Expository Text Comprehension
____Independent   ____Instructional   ____Frustration Level
____Listening Potential

Types of Comprehension Questions: Check those that student needs to strengthen
____Main Idea   ____Sequencing   ____Cause and Effect   ____Details
____Drawing Conclusions   ____Inference   ____Vocabulary/Concepts
____Determining Author's Point of View   ____Summarizing

Miscue Analysis: Level of reading passage _____

Graphophonic _____

_____

Syntax _____

_____

Semantic _____

_____

Reading Behaviors for which student needs instruction as indicated by the Reading Behaviors Checklist (see Appendix B) and teacher observations.

BEFORE READING _____

_____

DURING READING _____

_____

AFTER READING _____

_____

(continued)

Literacy Profile for Primary Grades (continued)

	Mastered	Satisfactory	Unsatisfactory
Knowledge of Concepts of Print			
Knowledge of Alphabetic Principle			
Knowledge of Phonemic Awareness			
Knowledge of Phonetic Analysis			

Consonants
  Initial
  Medial
  Final			

Short vowels			

Long vowels
  Vowel teams
  Blends
  Digraphs
  Diphthongs			

Knowledge of Structural Analysis
  Inflectional endings
  Compound words
  Contractions
  Prefixes
  Suffixes			

Knowledge of Syllabication			

(continued)

Literacy Profile for Primary Grades (continued)

Particular reading interests _____

_____

_____

What the student perceives as his or her difficulties with reading

_____

_____

_____

Writing Sample

Narrative: Topic _____

	4	3	2	1
Meaning				
Development				
Organization				
Language Use				
Mechanics				

Expository: Topic _____

	4	3	2	1
Meaning				
Development				
Organization				
Language Use				
Mechanics				

Teacher's Comments _____

_____

_____

Literacy Profile Progress Chart for Primary Grades

Student	Beginning of Year	Middle of Year	End of Year
Sorts letters			
Names letters			
Uppercase			
Lowercase			
Matches letters with sound			
Can alphabetize by first letter			
Forms letters correctly			
Sorts words			
Reads sight words			
Reads family words			
Makes words			
Spells words			
Reads left to right			
Reads top to bottom			
Reads phrases fluently			
Reads sentences fluently			
Reads short paragraph fluently			
Can locate words within a passage			
Can retell a short story			
Beginning			
Middle			
End			
Can summarize			
Can decode			
Can use picture clues			
Can use context clues			

Literacy Profile for Intermediate Grades

Name _____ Grade _____ Year _____

Standardized Test Scores:

Vocabulary ____Raw Score ____Percentile ____Stanine
____Grade Equivalent

Comprehension ____Raw Score ____Percentile ____Stanine
____Grade Equivalent

Reading Total ____Raw Score ____Percentile ____Stanine
____Grade Equivalent

Qualitative Reading Inventory:

Word Recognition
____Independent ____Instructional ____Frustration Level

Narrative Text Comprehension
____Independent ____Instructional ____Frustration Level
____Listening Potential

Expository Text Comprehension
____Independent ____Instructional ____Frustration Level
____Listening Potential

Types of Comprehension Questions: Check those that student needs to strengthen
____Main Idea ____Sequencing ____Cause and Effect ____Details
____Drawing Conclusions ____Inference ____Vocabulary/Concepts
____Determining Author's Point of View ____Summarizing

Miscue Analysis: Level of reading passage _____

Graphophonic _____

_____

Syntax _____

_____

Semantic _____

_____

(continued)

Literacy Profile for Intermediate Grades (continued)

Reading Behaviors for which student needs instruction as indicated by the Reading Behaviors Checklist (see Appendix B) and teacher observations.

BEFORE READING _____

_____

DURING READING _____

_____

AFTER READING _____

_____

	Mastered	Satisfactory	Unsatisfactory
Knowledge of Phonetic Analysis			
Consonants			
Medial vowels			
Blends			
Digraphs			
Diphthongs			
Knowledge of Structural Analysis			
Inflectional endings			
Compound words			
Contractions			
Prefixes			
Suffixes			
Knowledge of Syllabication			

(continued)

Literacy Profile for Intermediate Grades (continued)

Particular reading interests _____

_____

_____

_____

What the student perceives as his or her difficulties with reading

_____

_____

_____

_____

Teacher's determination of student's reading difficulties

_____

_____

_____

_____

Guided Reading Checklists

Guided Reading Observation Checklist

Reader _____ Grade _____

Text _____

Readability Level _____   Date _____

+ yes   — no   blank space—not observed

_____reads with appropriate directionality

_____reads fluently

_____reads with intonation and expression

_____reads with regard for punctuation marks

_____reads with appropriate phrasing

_____attempts to decode unfamiliar words

_____uses context clues to determine unfamiliar words

_____uses picture clues or other visual clues to determine meaning

_____skips unfamiliar words

_____self-corrects while reading

_____rereads words, sentences, or phrases

_____asks questions

_____asks for assistance

_____makes a significant amount of word recognition errors to adjust
     readability level of text

Informational Text	Narrative Text
_____identifies major concepts	_____identifies and describes characters
_____makes generalizations	_____describes setting
_____locates specific details	_____sequences events
_____explains a process with appropriate organization	_____identifies problem and solution
_____summarizes content	_____retells story

Other significant observations _____

_____

_____

_____

Reading Behaviors Checklist

Name_____ Grade _____ Date_____

Directions: Read each statement carefully and think about what you do before, during, and after you read. Then circle the number that matches your response.

	Not at all	Sometimes	Always
Before reading a book or textbook:			
1. I look at and think about the cover and title of the book.	1	2	3
2. I also examine the back cover of the book.	1	2	3
3. I read the inside jacket of the book.	1	2	3
4. I ask questions about the book or cover.	1	2	3
5. I try to guess what the book is about.	1	2	3
6. I look at the pictures, charts, and graphs.	1	2	3
7. I read the headings or bold-print words.	1	2	3
8. I look in the book to see if there are words I can't read or I don't understand.	1	2	3
9. I think about what I already know about the topic.	1	2	3
Then while I'm reading:			
10. I try to picture in my mind what I am reading.	1	2	3
11. I stop and check to see if I understand what I am reading.	1	2	3
12. I ask questions about the confusing parts of the book.	1	2	3
13. I try to use context clues to read words I don't know.	1	2	3
14. I reread parts that are confusing to me.	1	2	3
15. I use pictures, charts, and graphs to help me understand what I am reading.	1	2	3

(continued)

The Guided Reading Kidstation Model: Making Instruction Meaningful for the Whole Class by E. Francine Guastello and Claire R. Lenz. © 2007 International Reading Association. May be copied for classroom use.

Reading Behaviors Checklist (continued)

	Not at all	Sometimes	Always
16. I stop and retell myself what I read so that I can remember.	1	2	3
17. I check to see if my guesses were right.	1	2	3
18. I raise questions and read to find the answers.	1	2	3

Then after I finish reading:

	Not at all	Sometimes	Always
19. I retell the story or explain the facts in my own words.	1	2	3
20. I summarize the story or selection.	1	2	3
21. I can explain the author's purpose.	1	2	3
22. I reread and find details.	1	2	3
23. I check my guesses to see if I was right.	1	2	3
24. I think about parts I liked and why I liked them.	1	2	3
25. I speak, draw, or write about my favorite parts.	1	2	3
26. I can relate the story to something else I have read.	1	2	3
27. I can create a new ending or part of the story.	1	2	3

Student Inventories

Student Interest Inventory

My name is _____. I am in class _____.

The thing I like most about my class is _____

_____.

My favorite subject in school is _____

because _____.

A subject that is hard for me is _____

because _____.

I know a lot about _____.

I would like to know more about _____.

After school, I _____

_____.

When I am with my friends, I _____

_____.

When I am alone and I have free time, I _____

_____.

The best book I ever read was _____.

I like books about _____.

When I grow up I want to be _____

because _____.

The best thing I ever did with my family was _____

_____.

My favorite television show is _____.

My favorite movie is _____.

My favorite sport is _____.

I am happiest when _____.

Reading Inventory

Check off the topics you like to read about. If you don't see a topic, add it to the list.

Name _____ Grade _____

I like to read about

___sports	___hobbies	___comics	___fishing
___nature	___knitting/sewing	___history	___space
___cooking	___people/biographies	___legends	___fashion
___mysteries	___science fiction	___animals	___myths
___music	___adventure stories	___computers	___food
___folk tales	___funny stories	___natural wonders	___dreams
___occupations	___believe-it-or-not stories	___how-to books	_____

I really enjoy reading

___with others   ___with an adult   ___by myself

I like to read when _____.

I like to read   ___silently to myself   ___aloud so I can hear what I am reading

I like when   ___people read to me   ___I can listen to stories on tape

I don't like to read that much because (check as many answers that are true for you)

___I don't always like the topics

___I find reading some books very hard

___I don't know what to do when I can't read some words

Other reasons: _____

_____

_____

_____

_____

Thinking About Reading and Writing

My name is _____. I am in class _____.

I am a good reader because I _____.

I am a good writer because I _____

_____.

When I come to a word I can't read, I _____.

When I come to a word I can't spell, I _____.

When I don't understand what I am reading, I _____.

When I don't know what to write about, I _____

_____.

One thing that it is hard for me to do in reading is _____

_____.

One thing that it is hard for me to do in writing is _____

_____.

My family thinks reading is _____.

My family reads _____.

My favorite time and place for reading is _____.

My family thinks writing is _____.

My family writes _____.

My favorite time and place for writing is _____.

My favorite kind of book to read is _____.

My favorite kind of writing is _____.

My favorite reading activity is _____.

My favorite writing activity is _____.

The best book I ever read is _____.

The best piece I ever wrote is _____.

I think my biggest problem with reading is _____.

I think my biggest problem with writing is _____.

Student Learning and Modality Preference

Circle all of the items that describe you.

This Is How I Like to Learn

1. I like to work alone.
2. I like to work with another student.
3. I like to learn with a student and the teacher.
4. I like to work with the teacher or an adult.
5. I like to learn in a small group.
6. I can learn in most of these ways.

This Is How I Like the Room Where I Work to Be

1. I like the room to have bright lights.
2. I like soft lighting.
3. Either bright or soft light is fine.
4. I can study with music playing or other sounds around me.
5. I like the room to be quiet.
6. I can work in sound or quiet.
7. When I am learning something new, I like the room to be in a warm place.
8. When I am learning something new, I like the room to be cool.
9. I can learn in warm or cool places.
10. When I do my homework or study, I like to sit at a desk.
11. When I do my homework or study, I like to lie on a bed, rug, or the couch.
12. It doesn't matter to me where I study.

This Is What I Do When My Teacher Gives Me an Assignment

1. I complete the assignments as I have been told.
2. I need to take a break and then get back to the assignment.
3. Sometimes I complete the assignment all at once. At other times I take breaks.

(continued)

The Guided Reading Kidstation Model: Making Instruction Meaningful for the Whole Class by E. Francine Guastello and Claire R. Lenz. © 2007 International Reading Association. May be copied for classroom use.

Student Learning and Modality Preference (continued)

4. When the teacher gives me an assignment, I like to use my own ideas and set a date to complete it.

5. I like to follow the teacher's exact directions when I complete an assignment.

6. I can complete the assignment either way.

7. I need to complete the assignment my own way and in my own time. Sometimes I need to be reminded to get it done.

8. I want to get started right away to complete the assignment.

9. I usually need someone to get me started and help me to finish the project.

This Is the Way I Think

1. When I close my eyes and think of a cat, I see a picture of the cat.

2. When I close my eyes, I see the letters in the word cat.

3. I see both the picture and the letters.

4. I cannot see either the picture or the letters.

5. I like it when the teacher begins a lesson with a big picture, main idea, or story.

6. I like it when the teacher lists the facts and details.

7. It doesn't matter to me how the lesson is started.

8. I need time to think about the question and answers, and then I plan my work.

9. I answer questions right away and get started on my work right away.

10. I can answer about something new and difficult either way.

This Is How I Like to Present New Information or an Assignment

1. I like to speak about what I have learned.

2. I like to write a report that the teacher reads.

3. I like to make something and explain what I learned.

4. I like to take a test.

5. I would rather do a project with a short report.

6. I like doing a project with a speaking presentation.

The Guided Reading Kidstation Model: Making Instruction Meaningful for the Whole Class by E. Francine Guastello and Claire R. Lenz. © 2007 International Reading Association. May be copied for classroom use.

Learning Modalities Inventory

What Is the Best Way for Me to Learn?

Auditory Memory

Teacher's Directions: Please listen to the letters that I will say to you. When I say "begin," please write the letters that you hear next to each line.

Practice: A. c d o   B. m r h

1. d l b
2. c g h m
3. r j h x p
4. z l r t o q
5. n o w y p l j
6. n s j k t z q i

Visual Memory

Teacher's Directions: I will show you some letters on separate cards (you will need to create these cards with the letters listed below). Please look at the card. When I take the card away and say "begin," I want you to write the letters in the exact order that you saw them on the card.

Practice: A. f r b   B. t y z

Show each card for 5 seconds.

1. l f v
2. y z s r
3. m p w d n
4. h l j m p c
5. s p t m f b r
6. q k s d r m p t

Kinesthetic-Visual Memory

Teacher's Directions: I will show you some letters on cards (you will need to create these cards with the letters listed below). When I show you the card, write the letters in the air. When I take the card away, write the letters in the exact order on your paper.

Practice example: l v p

(*continued*)

Learning Modalities Inventory (continued)

1. v m t
2. l d j q
3. g r w n p
4. d t m k j k
5. f m w m h z x
6. p m s l g d c k

Kinesthetic-Auditory-Visual Memory

Teacher's Directions: I will say a nonsense word. Please repeat the word after me. Next, I will show you a card with the nonsense word (you will need to create these cards with the words listed below). Write it in the air. When I take the card away, write it on your paper.

Practice example: mag

1. wog
2. grep
3. ken no
4. nef les
5. rin o pin
6. si mo plas

Scoring: Determine the student's strongest modality or modalities by using the key below.

Satisfactory Achievement:

Grades 1–3:   3 or more correct
Grades 4–6:   4 or more correct

Planning Sheets

Planning Sheet for Guided Reading Groups

Group _____   Dates _____ to _____

Students' Names   Books Used

1._____   _____

2._____   _____

3._____   _____

4._____   _____

5._____

6._____

7._____

Skills and Strategies _____

_____

_____

_____

_____

_____

_____

_____

_____

_____

Anecdotal Comments of Students' Progress _____

_____

_____

_____

_____

_____

_____

_____

_____

Planning Sheet for Guided Reading Activity

Title _____

Author _____

Genre _____

Comprehension Skill _____

Vocabulary words suggested by author and identified by student

_____

_____

Kidstation One

What word recognition, vocabulary skills, or both do the students need to develop their understanding and application of the words? Or what literal comprehension skill needs to be developed?

_____

_____

Kidstation Two

What questions might you ask the students to determine their understanding of the literature using inference and implicit comprehension? Or the comprehension skill of _____ was the focus of this lesson. What activities can you develop so that students can respond to the literature?

_____

_____

Kidstation Three

What activities will be used to allow students to elaborate on the ideas of this story?

_____

_____

Extension activities could be multidisciplinary and include art projects as well. They can be related to but are not limited to the comprehension skill.

Directions
and Reproducibles
for Kidstation Activities

Vocabulary Quilt

Materials: Two pieces of light-color construction paper (different colors), scissors, text, and thesaurus

Directions (Note that directions can vary depending on the skill the teacher chooses to develop):
1. Cut one large square from each piece of paper.
2. Take one square and fold it in half. Cut it in half from the creased side to the open side but not all the way through. Leave about 1/4 of an inch from the end. Unfold the square.
3. Turn the square around, crease it, and follow the same procedure.

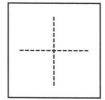

4. Now place this cut piece over the second square and glue the two pieces together around the edges only.
5. Next, gently take the tips of the cut piece and pull them back away from the center of the paper and crease them down.
6. In the center of the bottom square, write the new vocabulary word.
7. Find the sentence in the text containing the new vocabulary word and write it on the top right flap. Then explain what it means in that sentence.
8. Next, use the thesaurus to find five synonyms for the word and write them on the top left flap.
9. On the bottom left flap, write five antonyms.
10. On the bottom right flap, write a sentence of your own using your new vocabulary word.
11. When you are finished, "sew" (or tape) your square to your classmates' squares to form the vocabulary quilt.

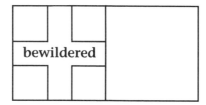

bewildered

The Slider

Materials: Paper, notecards, scissors, picture cards
(see page 119)

Directions:
1. Cut a 1" x 8" strip of paper and vertically print on it
   initial consonants and consonant blends.
2. On a 3" x 5" note card, write a word family and leave
   room on either side of it.
3. On the left side of the note card, cut a 1¼" slit on the
   top of the card and at the bottom. Slide the vertical
   strip through the slits so each letter or blend appears
   before the word family and creates a word.
4. Have students cut out the pictures that illustrate the
   words (see page 119). Ask students to pronounce each
   word using the slider and then show the corresponding
   picture. This part of the activity can be reversed so that
   students begin with the pictures and then create the
   words using the slider.

ig

B

F

D

W

P

Tw

(continued)

The Slider (continued)

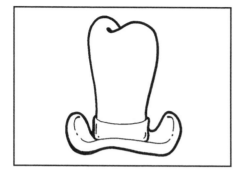 

Seek and Find

Directions: The following seek-and-find questions are based on the book *Ice Walk* by Cass Hollander. Let's see how well you can find these words in the story.

1. Find the five contractions in the story and write the two words that make each contraction.

   _____   _____
   _____   _____
   _____   _____
   _____   _____
   _____   _____

2. Write the five compound words in the story.

   _____   _____
   _____   _____
   _____

3. Find the antonyms for the following words, which can be found in the story.
   dangerous _____   liquid _____
   tense _____   frozen _____

4. While describing the ice on the river, the man said, "It's as solid as land." What do you think he meant by that?

   _____
   _____

5. Find synonyms for the following words.
   boat _____   targeted _____
   alerted _____   called _____
   terrible _____   moaning _____

6. Find the seven past tense verbs in the story.

   _____   _____   _____
   _____   _____   _____
   _____

7. Find the four proper nouns in the story.

   _____   _____
   _____   _____

Word Origin: "ology"

Materials: Puzzle and puzzle pieces, scissors

Directions:
1. Provide students with the puzzle pieces containing the names of different sciences ending in "ology" and have them cut out each piece.
2. Allow students to use their science texts and the Internet if necessary to determine the definition of each science name.
3. Have students record their answers in their notebooks. Then students should use their answers to match the puzzle pieces to the definitions on the puzzle (see page 122).

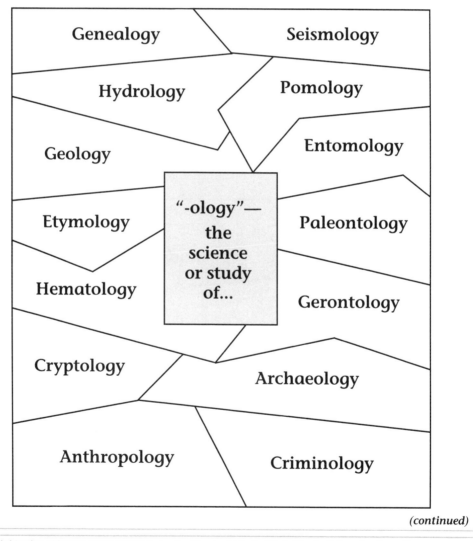

Genealogy

Seismology

Hydrology

Pomology

Geology

Entomology

"-ology"—
the
science
or study
of...

Etymology

Paleontology

Hematology

Gerontology

Cryptology

Archaeology

Anthropology

Criminology

(continued)

Word Origin: "ology" (continued)

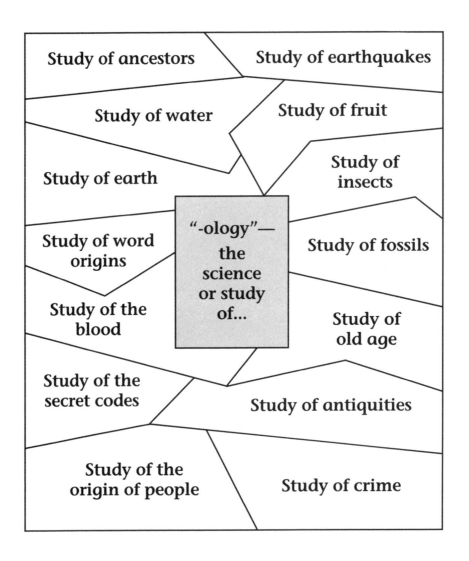

Story Grammar Wheel Base

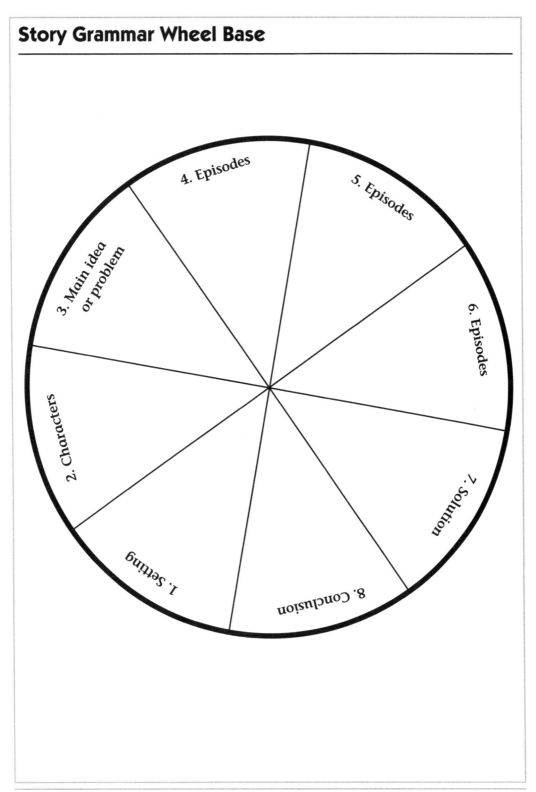

The Guided Reading Kidstation Model: Making Instruction Meaningful for the Whole Class by E. Francine Guastello and Claire R. Lenz. © 2007 International Reading Association. May be copied for classroom use.

Story Grammar Wheel Overlay

Setting—
Where and when does
the story take place?

Conclusion—
How does the
story end?

Solution—
How is the problem solved?

Characters—
Who are the main
characters in the story?

Episodes/Events—
What are the important events
that take place in the story?
Write them in the order they
occurred.

Main Idea/Problem—
What is the main idea of the story OR
What is the problem in the story?

Story Grammar Wheel

Evaluations

Oral Presentation Evaluation

Student _____

Grade _____   Date _____

Topic _____

Type of Presentation _____

Time Limit _____

Evaluation Criteria	Point Range	Self-Evaluation	Teacher Evaluation	Parent Evaluation
Mechanics				
• Voice quality (projection)	0–10			
• Pronunciation (correctness)	0–10			
• Diction (endings)	0–10			
Delivery				
• Audience contact (eyes)	0–10			
• Poise	0–10			
• Sincerity (ownership of speech)	0–10			
• Variations of tone (high–low)	0–10			
Interpretation				
• Appropriate gestures or props	0–10			
• Effectiveness or emphasis	0–10			
• Overall realism	0–10			
Total				

(*continued*)

Oral Presentation Evaluation (continued)

Teacher's Comments _____

_____

_____

_____

_____

_____

_____

_____

_____

_____

_____

Parent's Comments _____

_____

_____

_____

_____

_____

_____

_____

_____

_____

Presentation Goals _____

_____

_____

_____

_____

_____

_____

_____

_____

_____

Multimedia Presentation Four-Point Rubric

Student _____

Date _____ Grade _____

Title of Presentation _____

Type of Presentation _____

	4	3	2	1
Content of Presentation	The project flows well, keeps the attention of the audience, and contains relevant information to support ideas.	The project flows well and is somewhat interesting. It contains most of the details to support idea.	The majority of the project is disjointed, and the content is not sufficient to support ideas.	The project does not flow at all, is poorly constructed, and does not contain relevant information.
Language and Mechanics	The information is accurate; well-written; and complete with proper grammar, punctuation, and vivid language.	The majority of the text is accurate and uses proper grammar. The language use is clear and punctuation correct.	The project uses an acceptable amount of text. Language is only satisfactory. There are several errors in punctuation.	Information is missing. There is little use of vivid language and many errors in grammar and punctuation.

(continued)

Multimedia Presentation Four-Point Rubric (continued)

	4	3	2	1
Delivery	The speaker's pronunciation is clear, poised, fluent, uses gestures appropriately. The speaker demonstrates good eye contact. The speaker is not poised, there are not enough gestures, and he or she relies on notes somewhat. The speaker is easy to listen to.	The speaker's pronunciation is understandable, but there is some hesitation, not enough eye contact. The speaker is not poised, there are not enough gestures, and he or she relies on notes somewhat. The speaker is easy to listen to.	The speaker's pronunciation is fair, but there is hesitation and little eye contact. The speaker is unfocused and relies on reading from slides too much. He or she is not easy to listen to.	The speaker's pronunciation is very poor, very choppy, there is no eye contact, and he or she reads from slides. The speaker is not pleasant to listen to.
Graphics and Images	The images used to enhance the text are most effective and placed appropriately.	The images used to enhance the text are satisfactory. The placement of images is good.	The images used to enhance the text are ineffective and not placed appropriately.	There were no images or graphics used.

Content of Presentation _____   14–16 Excellent   11–13 Very Good   9–10 Satisfactory

Language and Mechanics _____   Delivery _____   Graphics and Images _____

Total Score _____   Parent's Signature _____   Date _____

Additional Resources

Kidstation One

Word Recognition and Phonics

Tripod, Phonemic Awareness for Young Language Learners
members.tripod.com/~ESL4Kids/phonics.html

Provides several strategies for developing phonological and phonemic awareness through songs and games

Enchanted Learning's Long A Alphabet Activities
www.enchantedlearning.com/themes/letters/longa.shtml

Provides alphabet worksheets for each letter of the alphabet and long and short vowel sounds

Starfall.com
www.starfall.com

Provides phonics activities for young children and books that can be downloaded from which children can practice reading specific phonograms

Developing Rhyming Abilities

Enchanted Learning's Rebus Rhymes
www.enchantedlearning.com/Rhymes.html

Includes young children's rhymes with pictures that can be used for phonological awareness and can be used for shared reading

Scholastic's Building Language for Literacy
teacher.scholastic.com/activities/bll/index.htm

Includes many resources for literacy activities including the following: alphabet recognition, early reading, guided reading, literature, phonemic awareness, assessment, and much more, and also includes online literacy activities for elementary children

Vocabulary

Interesting Things for ESL Students
www.manythings.org

Provides a variety of vocabulary building activities for English-language learners but may be used by other students as well

Edu4Kids
www.edu4kids.com/index.php?page=15

Focuses on practice for using context clues and other vocabulary reinforcement activities

Nanana.com
www.nanana.com/vocabulary.html

Contains a number of vocabulary games and puzzles, as well as a number of links to other vocabulary sites

Funbrain's What's the Word? The Reading and Vocabulary Game
www.funbrain.com/vocab/index.html

Includes an excellent selection of vocabulary games

Kidstation Two

Early Childhood Education

Stories to Grow By
www.storiestogrowby.com

Includes stories from a multitude of cultures

Sesame Street's Story Corner
www.sesameworkshop.org/sesamestreet/?scrollerId=stories

Contains stories, games, music, and activities appropriate for developing literacy skills for preschool and primary-age students

Lil' Fingers
www.lil-fingers.com

Includes storybooks for toddlers

Children's Storybooks Online
www.magickeys.com/books/index.html

Includes illustrated children's books for children of all ages

StoryPlace
www.storyplace.org/preschool/preschool.asp?themeID=1

A great place for stories (as the name suggests) and follow-up activities

PBS Kids Between the Lions Stories
pbskids.org/lions/stories.html

Contains stories, games, songs, printable downloads, and teacher and parent resources

Chateau Meddybemps Beantime Stories
www.meddybemps.com/5.1.html

Includes interesting stories, games, and ideas for parents and teachers

eduScapes Beyond the Books: Reading, Technology, and Standards
www.eduscapes.com/sessions/bike

Includes web-based reading and literacy units that address common reading standards and benchmarks, and sample themes by grade level

Figurative Language

Alliteration

Adobe Digital Kids Club: Alliteration poem
www.adobe.com/education/digkids/lessons/alliteration.html

Allows students to write an alliteration-style poem and then illustrate and publish the poem using Photoshop

Analogies

Fact Monster Analogy of the Day
www.factmonster.com/cgi-bin/analogy

Provides analogy quizzes, as well as facts about a variety of topics such as seasonal themes

Puzz.com's 1001 Best Puzzles
www.puzz.com/1001/analogies.htm

Provides anagrams, analogies, riddles, cryptograms, and other puzzles

Quia Vocab/Word Knowledge
www.quia.com/cb/7146.html

Provides a wealth of materials for teachers and students, among them are games on analogies

Idioms

English Daily
www.englishdaily626.com/idioms.html

Lists many types of idioms

Funbrain.com's Paint by Idioms Game
www.funbrain.com/idioms

Provides games for students to play with idioms and choose different themes such as animals, moods, and body parts

ESL Idiom Page
www.eslcafe.com/idioms

Especially helpful for English-language learners and provides idioms with their meanings

Metaphors and Similes

Pegasus, Metaphors & Similies
pegasus.cc.ucf.edu/%7Ebo236112/simile.htm

Provides teachers with an introduction to metaphors and similes, pictures, activities, English language arts standards, and references to additional websites

Personification

Poetry as We See It
library.thinkquest.org/J0112392/index.html

Defines personification and other poetry terms, as well as provides examples of each type of poem

Kidstation Three

Graphic Organizers

Scholastic's Graphic Organizers for Reading Comprehension
teacher.scholastic.com/lessonplans/graphicorg

Provides graphic organizers for organizational patterns, reading comprehension, story elements, and assessment

Enchanted Learning's Graphic Organizers
www.enchantedlearning.com/graphicorganizers

Provides a large number of various types of graphic organizers to download for reinforcement of reading skills, organizing research reports, writing book reports, creating concept maps, and making flow charts

edHelper.com Graphic Organizers
www.edhelper.com/teachers/graphic_organizers.htm

Presents graphic organizers in categories: general, sorting, graphs and charts, sequencing, storytelling, miscellaneous, K-W-L (what I Know, what I Want to know, what I Learned), and K-W-H-L (what I Know, what I Want to know, How I Learned), and also provides a useful introduction to graphic organizers

Houghton Mifflin Education Place Graphic Organizers
www.eduplace.com/graphicorganizer

Provides over 38 different types of graphic organizers, including those addressing problem solving, and can also be printed in Spanish

MasterMinds Publishing Graphic Organizers
www.graphicorganizers.com/reading.html

Provides graphic organizers that can be accessed by curriculum area, and categories of graphic organizers include hierarchic, story grammar, character analysis, comparison and contrast, cause and effect, sequences, and questions

Schools of California Online Resources for Education (S.C.O.R.E.) Graphic Organizers
www.sdcoe.k12.ca.us/score/actbank/torganiz.htm

Includes many useful graphic organizers, as well as information on journaling, rubrics, and literature

Learning Point Associates Graphic Organizers
www.ncrel.org/sdrs/areas/issues/students/learning/lr1grorg.htm

Gives descriptions of K-W-L-H technique, anticipation and reaction guide, and several other organizers, such as a spider map, cycle map, problem and solution outline, and network tree

WriteDesign Online Graphic Organizers
www.writedesignonline.com/organizers/comparecontrast.html#cc
matrix

Includes several different graphic organizers, as well as links to other sites with graphic organizers and other topics in literacy

abc teach Graphic Organizers
www.abcteach.com/directory/researchreports/graphic_organizers

Has a variety of graphic organizers to download with descriptions of how they can be used, and also includes resources for lesson planning, literacy strategies, and ideas for writing research reports

Kidstation Four

Creating Class Websites

myschoolonline
myschoolonline.com

Allows you to make your own website in approximately five minutes

Homestead
www.homestead.com/?s_cid=M130064B

Shows you how to make your own website inexpensively in three easy steps

teachers.net
teachers.net/sampler

Helps teachers make a class website

REFERENCES

Anderson, C. (2000). *How's it going? A practical guide to conferring with student writers*. Portsmouth, NH: Heinemann.

Antonacci, P.A. (2000). Reading in the zone of proximal development: Mediating literacy development in beginner readers through guided reading. *Reading Horizons, 41*(1), 19–33.

Bloom, B.S. (1984). *Taxonomy of educational objectives*. Boston: Allyn & Bacon.

Booher-Jennings, J. (2006). Rationing education in an era of accountability. *Phi Delta Kappan, 87*, 756–761.

Brown, G.T. (2004). Teachers' conceptions of assessment: Implications for policy and professional development. *Assessment in Education Principles, Policy and Practice, 11*, 301–318.

Burmark, L. (2002). *Visual literacy: Learn to see, see to learn*. Alexandria, VA: Association for Supervision and Curriculum Development.

Capper, C.A., Hafner, M.M., & Keyes, M.W. (2001). Moving beyond "good/bad" student accountability measures: Multiple perspectives of accountability. *Journal of School Leadership, 11*, 204–216.

Ceprano, M.A., & Garan, E.M. (1998). Emerging voices in a university pen-pal project: Layers of discovery in action research. *Reading Research and Instruction, 38*(1), 31–56.

Churchill, K., Durdel, J., & Kenney, M. (1998). *Hear it, feel it, see it: Improving early reading acquisition through a multisensory phonemic awareness approach* (Doctoral dissertation, Saint Xavier University, 1998). (ERIC Document Reproduction Service No. ED420049)

Clay, M. (1993). *An observation survey for early literacy achievement*. Portsmouth, NH: Heinemann.

Dymock, S.J. (1998). A comparison study of the effects of text structure training, reading practice, and guided reading on reading comprehension. *National Reading Conference Yearbook, 47*, 90–102.

Ediger, M. (2000). *Grouping pupils for instruction*. Kirksvill, MO: Truman State University.

Felder, R.M., & Brent, R. (2005). Understanding student differences. *Journal of Engineering Education, 94*(1), 57–72.

Ford, M.P., & Optiz, M.F. (2002). Using centers to engage children during guided reading time: Intensifying learning experiences away from the teacher. *The Reading Teacher, 55*, 710–717.

Fountas, I.C., & Pinnell, G.S. (1996). *Guided reading: Good first teaching for all children*. Portsmouth, NH: Heinemann.

Fountas, I.C., & Pinnell, G.S. (2001). *Guiding readers and writers, grades 3–6: Teaching comprehension, genre, and content literacy*. Portsmouth, NH: Heinemann.

Guastello, E.F. (2003, March). Multi-media and oral presentation skills: A perfect match! *Today's Catholic Teacher*, 16–19.

Guastello, E.F., & Lenz, C. (2005). Student accountability: Guided reading kidstations. *The Reading Teacher, 59*, 144–156.

Guastello, E.F., & Sinatra, R. (2001). Improving students' oral presentation skills through the use of technology and multi-media. *The Language and Literacy Spectrum, 11*, 5–17.

Gunning, T.G. (2006). *Assessing and correcting reading and writing difficulties* (3rd ed.). Boston: Allyn & Bacon.

Hadaway, N.L., Vardell, S.M., & Young, T.A. (2001). Scaffolding oral language development through poetry for students learning English. *The Reading Teacher, 54*, 796–806.

Haywood, H.C., Brown, A.L., & Wingenfeld, S. (1990). Dynamic approaches to psychoeducational assessment. *School Psychology Review, 19*, 411–422.

Hornsby, D. (2000). *A closer look at guided reading.* Armadale, VIC, Australia: Eleanor Curtain.

International Reading Association & National Council of Teachers of English. (1996). *Standards for the English language arts.* Newark, DE; Urbana, IL: Authors.

Isbell, R.T., & Exelby, B. (2001). *Early learning environments that work.* Beltsville, MD: Gryphon House.

Ivey, G. (1999). A multicase study in the middle school: Complexities among young adolescent readers. *Reading Research Quarterly, 34*, 172–192.

LaMere, R., & Lanning, J.L. (2000). An important aspect of guided reading: Books galore! Classroom Connections. *Council Connections, 5*(3), 26–28.

Mathews, M.M. (1966). *Teaching to read: Historically considered.* Chicago: University of Chicago Press.

Mohr, K.A.J. (1998). Teacher talk: A summary analysis of effective teachers' discourse during primary literacy lessons. *Journal of Classroom Interaction, 33*(2), 16–23.

Morrow, L. (2005). *Literacy development in the early years: Helping children read and write.* Boston: Allyn & Bacon.

National Institute of Child Health and Human Development. (2000). *Report of the National Reading Panel. Teaching children to read: An evidence-based assessment of the scientific research literature on reading and its implications for reading instruction* (NIH Publication No. 00-4769). Washington, DC: U.S. Government Printing Office.

Ogle, D. (1986). K-W-L: A teaching model that develops active reading of expository text. *The Reading Teacher, 39*, 564–570.

Page, M.S. (2002). Technology enriched classrooms: Effects on students of low socioeconomic status. *Journal of Research on Technology in Education, 34*, 389–410.

Palincsar, A.S., & Brown, A.L. (1984). Reciprocal teaching of comprehension-fostering and comprehension-monitoring activities. *Cognition and Instruction, 2*, 117–175.

Paris, S.G., & Hoffman, J.V. (2004). Reading assessment in kindergarten through third grade: Findings from the center for the improvement of early reading achievement. *The Elementary School Journal, 105*, 199–218.

Pearson, P.D. (2002). American reading instruction since 1967. In N.B. Smith (Ed.), *American Reading Instruction* (Special ed., pp. 419–486). Newark, DE: International Reading Association.

Perlmutter, J., & Burrell, L. (2001). *The first weeks of school: Laying a quality foundation.* Portsmouth, NH: Heinemann.

Raphael, T. (1986). Teaching question answer relationships, revisited. *The Reading Teacher, 39*, 516–522.

Reutzel, D.R. (1998–1999). On balanced reading. *The Reading Teacher, 52*, 322–324.

Reutzel, D.R., & Cooter, R.B. (2003). *Strategies for reading assessment and instruction: Helping every child to succeed.* Upper Saddle River, NJ: Prentice Hall.

Roe, B.D., Smith, S.H., & Burns, P.C. (2005). *Teaching reading in today's elementary school* (9th ed.). Boston: Houghton Mifflin.

Schwartz, R.M. (2005). Decisions, decisions: Responding to primary students during guided reading. *The Reading Teacher, 58,* 436–443.

Shellard, E.G. (2003). Using assessment to support reading instruction. *Principals, 83*(2), 40–43.

Short, R.A., Kane, M., & Peeling, T. (2000). Retooling the reading lesson: Matching the right tools to the job. *The Reading Teacher, 54,* 284–295.

Simpson, J., & Smith, J. (2002). Guided reading develops fluency. *Literacy Today, 31*(10), 2–12.

Smith, N.B. (2002). *American reading instruction* (Special ed.). Newark, DE: International Reading Association.

Snow, C.E., Burns, M.S., & Griffin, P. (Eds.). (1998). *Preventing reading difficulties in young children.* Washington, DC: National Academy Press.

Spiegel, D.L. (1992). Blending whole language and systematic direct instruction. *The Reading Teacher, 46,* 38–44.

Stahl, S.A., & Kuhn, M.R. (2002). Making it sound like language: Developing fluency. *The Reading Teacher, 55,* 582–584.

Stipek, D. (2006). Accountability comes to preschool: Can we make it work for younger children? *Phi Delta Kappan, 87,* 740–747.

Strickland, D.S., Ganske, K., & Monroe, J.K. (2002). *Supporting struggling readers and writers: Strategies for classroom intervention 3–6.* Portland, ME: Stenhouse; Newark, DE: International Reading Association.

Teachers of English to Speakers of Other Languages. (1997). *ESL standards for pre-K–12 students.* Alexandria, VA: Author.

Tierney, R.J., & Readence, J.E. (2004). *Reading strategies and practices: A compendium* (6th ed.). Boston: Allyn & Bacon.

Tompkins, G.E. (2005). *Literacy for the 21st century: A balanced approach* (4th ed.). Upper Saddle River, NJ: Prentice Hall.

Villaume, S.K., & Brabham, E.G. (2001). Guided reading: Who is in the driver's seat? *The Reading Teacher, 55,* 260–263.

Vygotsky, L.S. (1978). *Mind in society: The development of higher psychological processes* (M. Cole, V. John-Steiner, S. Scribner, & E. Souberman, Eds. & Trans.). Cambridge, MA: Harvard University Press. (Original work published 1934)

Whitehead, D. (2002). "The story means more to me now": Teaching through guided reading. *Reading: Literacy and Language, 36*(1), 33–37.

Worthy, J., Broaddus, K., & Ivey, G. (2001). *Pathways to independence: Reading, writing, and learning in grades 3–8.* New York: Guilford.

INDEX

Note: Page numbers followed by *f* or *t* indicate figures or tables, respectively.

managing, 1–2, 12–23; need-based groupings, 19; Planning Sheet for, 114; skill-based groupings, 19; testimony, 11; types of groupings, 18–20
GUNNING, T.G., 13, 19, 138

H
HADAWAY, N.L., 59, 138
HAFNER, M.M., 47, 137
HARCOURT HORIZONS, 62, 80; summary chart of accomplishments, character traits, and values for Patrick Henry, 62, 62f; word pyramid for Benjamin Franklin, 62–63, 63f
HAYWOOD, H.C., 13, 138
HENNESSY, B.G., 37
HENRY, PATRICK: summary chart of accomplishments, character traits, and values for, 62, 62f
HISPANICS, 5
HOFFMAN, J.V., 15, 138
HOLLANDER, CASS, 36
HOLOCAUST, 90
HORNSBY, D., 22, 138

I
IDIOMS: resources for, 134
IMPLEMENTATION: five-day model, 48t, 48–49, 85; five-day model incorporated into four-week cycle, 54, 54t
INCLUSION CLASSES, 89
INDEPENDENT READING, 26–28, 27f
INDEPENDENT WORK, 86
INFORMAL ASSESSMENTS, 16–17, 17t
INFORMED DECISION MAKING, 12–23
INNER-CITY SCHOOLS, 89
INTEREST INVENTORIES, 15, 106
INTERMEDIATE GRADES: ideas for kidstations for, 76t–77t; Literacy Profile for, 98–100. See also grades 4–6
INTERNATIONAL READING ASSOCIATION (IRA), ix, 1–2, 4, 32, 35, 41, 43, 45, 138
INVENTORIES, 105–112; Reading Inventory, 14–15, 107; Student Interest Inventory, 15, 106; Student Learning and Modality Preference,

109–110; Thinking About Reading and Writing, 108
IRA. *See* International Reading Association
ISBELL, R.T., 31, 138
IVEY, G., 4, 78, 138, 139

J–K
JAMES, KARI, 70
K-W-L CHARTS, 38
KANE, M., 4, 139
KENNEY, M., 32, 137
KERR, JUDITH, 67
KEYES, M.W., 47, 137
KIDS MYSTERIES (MYSTERY NET), 74
"KIDSTATION" (TERM), 31
KIDSTATIONS, ix; activities for, 21–22, 84–85, 116–124; class arrangement for, 50, 51f; components of, 4–5; creating, 24–46; evolution of, 1–11; five-day model for, 48t, 48–49, 54, 54t, 85; four-week cycle, 54, 54t; ideas for, 76t–77t; implementing, 47–60; model, ix, 4–5, 5–10, 83–91; preplanning activities for, 32–35; student response to, 90; types of, 31–46; using basal readers with, 61–67; using content area textbooks with, 75–82; using leveled texts with, 70–75; using trade books with, 67–70
KIDSTATION ONE, 4, 10, 34, 35–40; day 2, 50–52; day 3, 52–53; day 4, 53; resources for, 131–132; using basal readers with, 62, 64–65; using content area textbooks with, 79, 80–81; using leveled texts with, 70–71, 73; using trade books with, 67–68
KIDSTATION TWO, 4–5, 10, 34, 41–43; day 3, 52–53; day 4, 53; resources for, 132–134; using basal readers with, 62–63, 65; using content area textbooks with, 79–80, 81; using leveled texts with, 71–72, 73–74
KIDSTATION THREE, 5, 10, 34, 43–44; day 4, 53; resources for, 134–136; using basal readers with, 64, 65–67; using content area textbooks with, 80, 81; using leveled texts with, 72, 74, 74f, 75f; using trade books with, 69